LONG-LIVED LADIES
and
MORE TUDOR TALES

Marie Sandeford

JOROBY BOOKS

By the same author:
The Second Sister
Tales of Tudor Women

First published in Great Britain in 2012
by Joroby Books, 15 Bridgewater Drive,
Great Glen, Leics. LE8 9DX

ISBN-10: 0 9534584 2 3
ISBN-13: 978 0 9534584 2 4

British Library Cataloguing in Publication Data
A catalogue record for this book is available from the
British Library

Printed and bound by CPI Group (UK) Ltd, Croydon, CR0 4YY

*Cover illustration: Lady Anne Herbert and her daughter, Lady
Anne Talbot (the sister and niece of Queen Katherine Parr)*

**'Fortune is to me sometyme a mother, sometyme a
stepdame'**
Window inscription by Anne Talbot, Buxton, 1570s

CONTENTS

Elizabeth of York

INTRODUCTION

From Bessy 'the Good' to 'Good Queen Bess'

"Would you have me imprison women like nuns in a convent?" said Queen Elizabeth I during one of the numerous times she scorned her male advisors. "A fine thing that would be!" Yet she was 'forever telling' a Spanish ambassador to England, Bishop de Quadra, that she 'yearns to be a nun and pass her time in a cell praying'.

Tales of in-fighting in nunneries during the reign of Elizabeth's father, King Henry VIII, included complaints that some of the nuns at Carrow Priory in Norwich were gabbling their prayers and singing hymns so quickly that they could hardly catch their breath. The older nuns said that the younger ones were too prone to gossip, and further moans were made about the ale being too weak. At Stainfield Priory in Lincolnshire, though, the singing was sometimes non-existent, as the nuns developed a tendency to stay up late at night and those who attended the early morning services in church were known to fall asleep in their choirstalls!

An early 16th-century ballad called *The Song of the Lady Bessy*, based on an oral tradition, appeared in written form during Queen Elizabeth's reign. It was about the beautiful and popular grandmother after whom she was named – Elizabeth of York, the first Tudor Queen. In one of its many verses, Elizabeth of York saw her father, King Edward IV, studying a book of magic one day. He showed her the horoscope he had drawn from this and 'predicted that she should be queen, and the crown would rest in her descendants'. Before then, though, Elizabeth had torn at her long, fair hair 'that shone as golden wire' when she experienced the chauvinism of her future stepfather-in-law, Lord Stanley, who believed that 'it is difficult to trust the secrecy of women, and many a man is brought to great woe by making them his confidantes'.

In 1502, the Tudor Court astrologer, William Parron, predicted that Elizabeth would live until she was eighty years old or more – a welcome prospect to the English people, who affectionately called their Queen, 'Elizabeth the Good'. Her kindness and gentleness made her far more popular than her husband, King Henry VII, as also did her Madonna-like beauty, in a kingdom still steeped in its medieval tradition of devotion to the Blessed Virgin Mary.

But when Elizabeth of York died in childbirth on her thirty-eighth birthday, in February 1503, Parron fled into exile, amid the heartfelt mourning for her. If she had lived to fulfil his prediction, what a benign - and even a restraining – influence she would have had for most of her son, Henry VIII's action-packed reign and what the Tudor writer, John Foxe, later summarized as its 'dangerous tempests'. Her son closely resembled her father, whose good looks, extrovert personality and over-fondness for 'pleasure, pastime and dalliance' had ultimately caused his early death. While the 'Golden Prince' Henry was a source of maternal pride, he was also, therefore, one of potential worry, and her own untimely death when he was only eleven was a great loss to him, as well as to Tudor England.

A hundred years separated Elizabeth of York's demise from that of her brilliantly learned and equally popular granddaughter, Elizabeth I. Such a century of change this proved to be, from the Catholic world and its shrines dedicated to the Virgin Mary, to the Protestant Elizabethan period with its cult of the 'Virgin Queen'.

Many Tudor women did live until eighty years old or more, one of them being Elizabeth I's faithful Welsh servant, Blanche Parry, who was eighty-two when she died in 1589. Blanche's memorial in Bacton Church, Herefordshire, shows an effigy of her in worship, as she kneels beside an effigy of the Queen in the same manner as people knelt, during her own youth, before images of the Virgin Mary. Her epitaph above these figures declares that 'wythe maeden queen a maede did ende my lyffe'. She served her royal mistress for so long that she had even seen the infant Elizabeth being rocked in her cradle.

Memorial to Blanche Parry at Bacton Church, Herefordshire

The famous and much-visited holy shrine of Our Lady of Walsingham, in Norfolk, reflected the troubled transition between early and late Tudor times. Elizabeth of York went on pilgrimage there while she was grieving after the deaths of two of her children in infancy. The shrine was a special favourite of her daughter-in-law, Queen Katharine of Aragon, and even Henry VIII visited there after Katharine gave birth to their short-lived son in 1511. The bejewelled statue of Our Lady of Walsingham was, however, 'brought to London ... at the King's commaundement' in 1538 and burnt at Chelsea with 'divers other images' from England and Wales 'that were used for common pilgrimages', so that 'the people should use noe more idolatrye unto them'.

Two years later, a complaint was made that, as yet, 'The said image is not well out of some of their heads'! A woman from Wells-next-the-Sea 'beside Walsingham, had imagined a miracle wrought by the image of Our Lady at Walsingham since it was brought to London'. This female victim of the changing times was punished by being 'set in the stocks at Walsingham on the market day with a paper about her head, "a reporter of false tales", and then sent ... round the town in a cart, the young people and boys casting snowballs at her'.

Amongst those 'divers other images' destroyed was one of great antiquity even by Tudor times, though this was not realized then. A statue from the healing well at Buxton in Derbyshire was believed to be of the Virgin Mary's mother, St Anne, and local tradition there told that it had been discovered 'miraculously' in the well, which has ever since been named after this patron saint of the disabled. The image was already over a thousand years old, however, when it was carted away unceremoniously to be burnt at Chelsea. It dated back to Roman, pre-Christian times when the Buxton well had been dedicated to a goddess called Arnemetia. The inscription ARNE, an abbreviated form of the goddess's name, had appeared on this Roman statue, but as a representation of St Anne, it had kept vigil for many centuries over a centre of Christian pilgrimage to which thousands of sick people had ventured in their hope for a cure. Buxton water was reputed to heal numerous ailments, help infertile women and cleanse and beautify the skin.

When this statue was removed from its shrine, the sick were also suddenly deprived of access to the bath and well at Buxton, which were 'lokkyd upp and sealyd ... that non schall enter to wasche ...' A letter written by the local knight, William Bassett, who received royal orders to take this action, referred to 'the ffonde trust that they dyd putt in those ymages'. To them, he perpetrated the sacrilege not only of personally taking down the Buxton statue and that of the Saxon female St Modwen at Burton-upon-Trent, but also defacing the 'tabernaculles and places where they dyd stande' and taking away 'cruchys, schertes and schetes, with wax offeryd, being thynges thatt dyd alure and intyse the yngnorantt pepull to the seyd offeryng'. In his zeal for sealing rather than healing, Bassett boasted of ordering 'no more offeryng' at Buxton 'tyll the kinges pleasure … be further knowen'.

Two decades passed before the reign of 'Good Queen Bess' began, but the local populace were still regarded as 'backward' in religion and patients who recovered were again leaving their crutches as a thanksgiving at the well. Elizabeth herself believed in the water's remedial powers and wrote of it lightheartedly as 'St Ann's sacred water'. She allowed her ailing cousin and captive, Mary Queen of Scots, to visit Buxton several times during the 1570s. An important part of any treatment there was daily physical exercise, and a game called 'troll-my-dames' was popular with 'ladies, gentlewomen and maids' if bad weather kept them indoors: this involved eleven holes 'in the end of a bench, into which to troul [roll] … bowles of lead, big, little or mean, or also of copper, tin, wood, either violent or soft, after their own discretion'.

Archery offered a more energetic activity for some female visitors too, though only for recreational purposes, unlike 'certain women' on the Isle of Wight who repelled an attempted landing by a French invasion force there in 1545, soon after Henry VIII's ship, the *Mary Rose*, sank during a war with France. These island women 'fought and shot their arrows so swiftly that they did incredible hurt, and ran like hares, and this because they hold these men [the French] here, in no estimation'.

A target of little estimation in her own home was a Tudor lady, who was born amid the upheavals before this incident, at a time when Henry VIII was half-way through his six wives. Catherine Gainsford came from a Surrey family and married Henry Needham of Nottinghamshire, who left her a wealthy widow with two sons and a daughter when she was forty. Along then came a 16th- century version of a toy-boy – John Kingston, of Lincolnshire, who was aged twenty-four, and bragged openly that he would 'marry this olde widdow' to pay his debts, and when he had buried her, he would 'marry a young wench and get children'. A family memoir disclosed with an air of glee what became of his 'designe': Catherine 'held him tug above 38 yeares and lived nearly 12 yeares after him'! Their only child was a daughter, Elizabeth Kingston, who died, aged twenty, when her son, Gervase Holles, who wrote the memoir, was 'yet an infant'. He clearly admired his grandmother much more than she was regarded by the husband whose life plan she thwarted because of her own longevity.

Holles described her as 'a woman of notable spirit' who was 'good and charitable', and despite being slightly built, she was blessed with 'a healthfull and happy constitution … shee never took phisicke in her life … and to hir last did read without spectacles'. She even kept all her teeth until the loss of 'one about 3 moneths and the other about 3 dayes before her last sicknes'! Until close to her end at the venerable age of eighty-nine, Catherine had always risen at six o'clock in the winter and before five in summer to see to the smooth running of her household.

Rather like her usual daily routine, another aspect of life stayed essentially the same amid all the ebb and flow of such eventful times - human nature itself, with its virtues and vices. When Catherine Gainsford was a baby, some of the long-established abbeys and priories in the kingdom still housed communities of nuns, and as part of the religious changes, small nunneries such as that at Crabhouse Priory in Norfolk had only recently ceased to exist. The Prioress of Crabhouse, Margaret Studefield, and her three nuns were all described as being 'of good name' in one report, but another alleged that they had caused a mini-population explosion in producing five illegitimate children between them – one each by the Prioress and two of the nuns, and two by the third nun, of which one was fathered by a priest! Good nuns and naughty nuns were mostly part of the past, however, by the time Catherine Gainsford was educated by her aunt, Cecily Wilsford, who was her mother's sister and belonged to a staunchly Protestant family from Kent. Several Wilsfords, including Cecily herself, went into exile abroad to avoid the risk of being burnt at the stake for their religious faith during the Catholic Queen Mary's reign. She returned to England in 1559, on the January day Queen Elizabeth was crowned.

Cecily had acquired a new status in exile, as the second wife of a Protestant clergyman, Edwin Sandys. Although clerical marriages were viewed by Queen Elizabeth and many of her people as one religious reform too far, this did not prevent her from recognizing Sandys' ability and in the spring she appointed him to lead a commission in Nottingham. This was probably when Cecily 'matched' her niece Catherine into the local Needham family. From 1575, aunt Cecily was more permanently near the same area, after her elderly husband became Archbishop of York. She was close enough to be aware of the debt-ridden, young second husband's derogatory comments about her niece as the 'olde widdowe', whom he only married for her money. But this situation preceded another, which was even more galling – a sexual scandal at Doncaster, South Yorkshire, which resulted in Archbishop Sandys being blackmailed!

One of the plotters was a former maid of Cecily's called Ann Sissons. She married an innkeeper, but she hardly proved to be mine genial hostess, at least not towards the Archbishop himself when he stayed overnight at her husband's Doncaster inn, during a journey in 1581. Sandys awoke to find that she had invited herself into bed with him, her husband contrived a show of fury when he reckoned to catch them and he brought in a third plotter as a witness, who was heavily in debt. The three extorted money from Sandys as the price of their silence over this episode, but they were later overheard gloating that blackmailing him was the best-paid business they had ever had. Much as he had wished to avoid scandal, in case it reflected on the Church, he sought the Queen's help over the matter and she ordered their imprisonment after all three plotters confessed their guilt.

While the downside of Tudor life clearly led to incidents which seemed incredible, but were nevertheless true rather than fictional, so too did the more joyous moments. A gem of an extract from an Elizabethan parish register in Leicester captured the mood of celebration at the wedding of a local woman, Ursula Russel, to Thomas Tilsye, neither of them tying the knot for reasons of money or property, or an arranged marriage by other people. Their motivation was love, and as Thomas was deaf, dumb, and could not read or write, the description of how he took his wedding vows is priceless: 'first, he embraced her with his arms, and tooke her by the hande, putt a ring on her finger, and layde his hande upon his hearte, and then upon her hearte ... And to show his continuance to dwell with her to his lyves ende, he did it by closing of his eyes with his handes, and digginge out of the earthe with his foote, and pulling as though he would ringe a bell ...'

What should have been wedding bells for a popular young Norfolk woman unfortunately tolled out instead as her death knell, after she died on the night before her wedding in 1591. Her epitaph in the village church at Ashmanhaugh states that she 'died godlye', but does not say why her passing was so ill-timed. She seems to have been free of premarital nerves, though, for it was not caused by any ailment or anxiety, but simply by a tragic accident during some youthful merry-making of a game of hide-and-seek, in which she hid in a heavy-lidded chest. After closing the lid, she was unable to reopen it from the dark interior.

Honor's epitaph also paid tribute to her that the world 'now her lyke doth lacke'. Being only eighteen, she was very much at the esteemed end of the 16th-century misogyny expressed in a sexist, ageist adage that a woman was an angel when she was ten years old, a saint at fifteen, a devil at forty and a witch at eighty! Although the medieval, Catholic world was such a distant one by the Elizabethan period, the old beliefs in superstition, magic and omens still persisted so much that these influenced the general outlook on life.

Even the 'Virgin Queen' became caught up in such beliefs, according to one Tudor tale. When Elizabeth, who had the appropriate star sign of Virgo, was yet several months away from her seventieth birthday, she appeared to

Table tomb of Honor Bacon, Ashmanhaugh Church, Norfolk

be in good health. A centenarian Welshwoman bequeathed her a piece of gold, which the Queen accepted from a member of her Privy Council one day. He told her that the old woman had claimed that as long as she herself had worn this gold on her body, death would elude her. 'Upon the confidence she had thereof', Elizabeth placed the gold on her neck ruff. A few days later, though, she fell ill and as her health worsened, two of her ladies found attached to her chair a card of 'the Queen of Hearts with a nail of iron knocked through the forehead', which they dared not to 'pull out, remembering that the like thing was reported to be used to others for witchcraft'.

Hope for the Queen's recovery then turned to despair, and soon the Tudor world lacked its 'most gracious Soveraigne Ladie Elizabeth'. And though she did not quite reach her three score years and ten, 'Good Queen Bess' was the longest lived of all the Tudor queens and kings. Her grandmother, Elizabeth of York's own paternal grandmother, Cecily, Duchess of York, did just survive till the age of eighty, dying later in the same month as her birthday in May 1495, as the first decade of Tudor times neared completion.

Between and beyond the two Tudor Queen Elizabeths, the women of their realm included others, young, old, rich and poor, who shared with Catherine Gainsford the distinction of being 'of notable spirit'. Some of their tales are recalled in this companion volume about Tudor women and the varied roles they played – long-forgotten stories besides others which are still well-known, for the very names of women such as Mother Shipton, Lady Anne Clifford, Bess of Hardwick and Katherine of Berain have become legends themselves.

CHAPTER 1

Four Lady Anne Cliffords

'Tribulation has been ... as a furnace to fine gold – a means of proving their virtue,' wrote Mary Queen of Scots in her *Essay on Adversity*. When Mary was escorted through spectacular Pennine scenery in Cumbria and upper Wensleydale, North Yorkshire, on her way to imprisonment at Bolton Castle in 1568, little could she have known that one day the route would be called 'Lady Anne's Highway', after a distant kinswoman whose dedication led to a remarkable story of triumph over tribulation.

Lady Anne Clifford nowadays also has a 100-mile walk, 'Lady Anne's Way' named in her honour, of which her Highway is one part. This trail, which begins at Skipton Castle in Yorkshire, where she was born in 1590 and ends at Brougham Castle, Cumbria, where she died aged eighty-six, links the many buildings she repaired and restored. Her achievement established her as one of the north of England's most outstanding women. A contemporary tribute paid to her was that she was 'absolute mistris of herself', a description which echoes the 'one mistress and no master here' of another royal kinswoman – Elizabeth I. The diminutive Lady Anne's indomitable character was probably influenced by her childhood meetings with the powerful old Queen during visits to the Tudor Court.

In contrast with these glimpses of female authority was a local, 19th-century summary of the men in her life: 'Anne Clifford had a bad father and two bad husbands.' Here were the sources of the tribulation which was to strengthen her resolute personality even more and ultimately become her personal 'furnace to fine gold'! Historians have sometimes tried to explain the conduct of her father George, 3rd Earl of Cumberland, by pointing out his deep sense of dejection when he was thwarted in love in his youth. One fact about

Lady Anne Clifford

Skipton Castle Gateway

this strange episode appears to have gone unnoticed, however – it was in itself a knock-on effect from a romantic incident involving a descendant of two other Lady Anne Cliffords.

A love poem penned by Earl George, and later set to music, is thought to have expressed his feelings for Gertrude Holles, an attractive girl from Haughton in Nottinghamshire. He was then in his late teens, and during the mid-1570s he followed the custom of the time by formally asking the girl's father for her hand in marriage. Friends and other members of Gertrude's family were in favour of the match, but her father, Sir William Holles, rebuffed all persuasions of the honour it would bring her and the Holles family. He declared that he would not stand cap in hand whenever he spoke to a son-in-law of higher rank, but would instead marry his daughter off to a gentleman with whom he could have 'friendship and conversation'. And so after turning down Earl George's offer for Gertrude, Sir William did just as he said, by arranging for her to become the wife of Walter Stanley of West Bromwich.

'All joys farewell,' seems to have been the Earl's lament over his loss of Gertrude. Her father's actions over her marriage take on a different, but far lesser known dimension, though, from the point of view of her family at the time. The troubles caused by another love-match were still so recent that Gertrude's father and her brother, Gervase, were not yet reconciled over this young man's elopement from Sherwood Forest with an heiress called Frances Frecheville. This haunt of Robin Hood in bygone days was situated between Haughton and Frances' home at Staveley in north Derbyshire. She was supposed to be returning there after her father, Peter Frecheville, summoned her home from a visit to Haughton, but she contrived for her escort of his servants to disappear over the brow of a hill. Forest trees then provided enough cover for Frances and her own maid to meet up with Gervase Holles, according to a prearranged plan, and they rode off to London, where the young couple were married.

Frances and her irate father were never reconciled. She had been regarded as 'one of the greatest matches in the north of England' because of her illustrious ancestry and substantial inheritance. But the elderly widower managed to disinherit his daughter completely, by remarrying very quickly and producing two sons with his new wife, a Yorkshirewoman called Margaret Key.

Both Earl George and Frances Frecheville could trace their family tree back to a royal marriage at the beginning of the Tudor period. King Henry VII's cousin, Anne St John, married Henry, 10th Lord Clifford, and they lived mostly at Barden Tower in Yorkshire's scenic Upper Wharfedale. One of their younger daughters, also named Anne, was Frances' great-grandmother. Like the Frecheville inheritance, that of the Clifford family was to be affected by Frances' Sherwood Forest elopement, for this contributed to the chain of events which changed Earl George's life after his ill-timed bid to marry Gertrude Holles.

While he was still on the rebound, he married seventeen year old Margaret Russell, daughter of the Earl of Bedford, but this arranged union followed something of a Clifford family tradition in proving to be unsuccessful. Earl George's neglect of his young bride began almost from the outset of their marriage. Their only surviving child was Lady Anne, and they separated when she was ten, the differences between them being very great – as she herself noted.

Lady Anne's closeness to her 'deare mother' brought much solace to both of them. However, she was the daughter too of a courtier and naval commander who wore Queen Elizabeth's glove in his hat, because he was so high in royal favour that he was appointed 'Queen's Champion' when Anne was still a baby. The deaths of both her older brothers, Francis and Robert, in infancy meant that she was also Earl George's 'sole and next lawful heir' from an early age – a status which she was to assert time and again throughout her life.

As part of expressing her right to the Clifford lands, Lady Anne gathered much information about her ancestors and wrote a family history of several generations of Cliffords through the Tudor period. She gave a glowing description of her great-great-grandmother, Anne St John, as a very sincere and devout, almost saint-like woman, who so excelled too at keeping house that she had tapestry hangings made, although these were rare in late 15th-century England. Some of the tapestries still survived in the Clifford family at the time of Lady Anne's memoirs in the 17th century.

Anne St John was sometimes known as Anne of Bletsoe, after the Bedfordshire village where she was born. Her aunt, Lady Margaret Beaufort, the most powerful woman in early Tudor England, had also been born there. Lady Margaret's fierce loyalty and devotion to her only son, Henry VII, included her extended family, the St Johns, who were descended from her own mother's first marriage. Occasionally she was even prepared to help them against the wishes of her precious royal son.

A Tudor tradition tells that Henry VII restored all the Clifford lands to Henry, Lord Clifford, 'chiefly … because he married the said King's cosin'. Certainly the Cliffords were in the position of having their properties confiscated by Elizabeth of York's father, Edward IV, during the 15th-century conflict of the Wars of the Roses and returned to them by her husband. Anne St John, the new Lady Clifford, acquired a spouse whose informal title, the 'Shepherd Lord', reflected his unusual upbringing after the loss of the family lands. His widowed mother had ensured his safety by entrusting him in secret disguise to the care of shepherds in Cumbria and the Border Country. She too was named Lady Margaret, and as she survived into the Tudor period, she had the satisfaction of seeing him regain his inheritance.

A chance meeting between the Shepherd Lord and Anne of Bletsoe is believed to be detailed in an early 16th-century ballad legend called *The Nute-Browne Mayde*. Anne's close kinship with Margaret Beaufort may have led to visits with her father to Lathom House in Lancashire, Aunt Margaret's home when she was the wife of Lord Stanley. From there, they could have visited the Shepherd Lord's mother and stepfather, Sir Lance Threlkeld, in the Lake District, where Anne came across her future lord in his plain, working attire as she rode out in the parkland surrounding Threlkeld Castle. The seemingly great social gulf between them was referred to in the twenty-first of the thirty-verse ballad:

> *'And though that I of ancestry*
> *A baron's daughter be,*
> *Yet have you proved how I you loved*
> *A squire of low degree;*
> *And ever shall, whatso befall,*
> *To die therefore anon(e);*
> *For, in my mind, of all mankind,*
> *I love but you alone.'*

Even the threat of the Shepherd Lord admitting to having a paramour 'whom I love more than you' did not deter the Maid's love for him in the ballad, which ended with him telling her:

> *'Now understand; to Westmoreland,*
> *Which is my heritage,*
> *I will you bring; and with a ring,*
> *By way of marriage,*
> *I will you take, and lady make,*
> *As shortly as I can;*
> *Thus have ye won an earl's son,*
> *And not a banished man.'*

The marriage produced two sons and four daughters, but the mention of a mistress in the ballad partly reflected reality. Lady Anne Clifford revealed in her family history that the Shepherd Lord was 'unkind' to his wife in her mature years and fathered several illegitimate children by another woman. He also preferred a reclusive existence at Barden Tower, studying the stars, rather than attending the Tudor Court with members of his family. The unhappy Lady Anne of Bletsoe sought royal advice on a possible separation from him. She was offered a place in Lady Margaret Beaufort's household if this went ahead, and she had a room at her aunt's main residence, Collyweston Palace in Northamptonshire, where she stayed when in need of a refuge. Her devout nature meant that she fitted in well with the pious ways of Lady Margaret. Perhaps one of the daughters recorded as accompanying her on visits to Collyweston was her young namesake, Anne, whose descendants were to include Frances Frecheville. *This* Lady Anne replaced her maiden name of Clifford with the similar-sounding surname of Clifton when she married into a Nottinghamshire family, who may have been part of Margaret Beaufort's wide network of connections in the Midlands.

Lady Margaret actively used her influence over the education of her great-nephew, the future 11th Lord Clifford. In total contrast to the childhood and youth on northern hills experienced by his father, the Shepherd Lord, he was brought up at Court with Prince Henry, with whom he formed a lasting friendship. Through this, an earldom was conferred on the Clifford family, as well as a second royal marriage. King Henry VIII created his childhood friend, the 11th Lord, as 1st Earl of Cumberland shortly after the death of the Shepherd Lord in 1523. The title of 'Lord Clifford' then went to the new Earl's eldest son, who was also called Henry and later destined to wed one of the King's nieces.

Tudor documents of the 1530s and Lady Anne Clifford's family memoirs referred respectfully to this royal bride as 'the Lady Eleanor's Grace'. She was betrothed at the age of fourteen to Lord Clifford soon before the death of her mother Mary, Dowager Queen of France and Duchess of Suffolk, the beautiful sister of Henry VIII, after whom he named his ship, the *Mary Rose*. Lady Eleanor Brandon and Lord Clifford were related to each other through Margaret Beaufort and the St Johns, but of greater significance was her Tudor descent, which placed her and any offspring of her Clifford marriage in the line of succession to the throne.

The King and all the Court attended the young couple's

wedding in the summer of 1535. Lady Anne Clifford noted in her family history that the ceremony took place at St Mary Overy Church in Southwark, where her own unfortunate parents married some forty years later. The splendid festivities for Lady Eleanor were at the London palace of her father, the Duke of Suffolk, and in the meantime her father-in-law ordered 'the great gallery at Skipton Castle, with the towers at the east end, in an octagonal form' to be built in honour of the marriage. When Lady Anne mentioned these 'stately additions', she wrote that they were then her personal residence during her frequent times at Skipton.

A list of items in Eleanor's wardrobe revealed many fine items, such as velvet shoes, sleeves 'of cloth of gold of the French fashion', kirtles of cloth of gold and crimson damask 'welted with crimson velvet', 'a purple satin gown, plated with five pieces of gold aglets, guarded with velvet, faced with green coloured sarcanet' and several gowns of black velvet, satin or damask. Perhaps she wore one of these black gowns when she was Chief Mourner at the funeral of Henry VIII's first wife, Katharine of Aragon, at Peterborough Cathedral early in 1536. This was the momentous year of three Tudor Queens: four months after Queen Katharine's death came the execution of Anne Boleyn and the King's marriage to Jane Seymour. It proved to be eventful for Eleanor too, with the birth of her first child, a son named Henry. But any chance of a happy, peaceful family life in the remote north, well away from the turbulent Tudor Court, was swiftly dashed in the autumn.

Early in October, a rebellion broke out in Lincolnshire and Eleanor's father led the royal army sent to suppress the rebels. Their grievances were far more widespread in the north, however, and the major uprising known as the Pilgrimage of Grace, which erupted in Yorkshire and other northern counties, was the most serious challenge to Henry VIII's rule. Eleanor's father-in-law and husband were amongst the few noblemen of the area who dared to resist the rebels, and were supported in their opposition by one of the Shepherd Lord's nephews, their cousin Christopher

Aske. In a vivid eye-witness account of drama concerning 'my Lady Eleanor's Grace, the King's niece', he called the rebel leader, Robert Aske, 'my ungracious brother'. Skipton Castle was besieged, but 'after two or three days, finding the castle impregnable', the rebels 'purposed to take' hostage Eleanor and her baby son, two of her sisters-in-law and 'other gentlewomen then at Bolton Abbey', about ten miles away. As a lady of royal blood, seventeen year old Eleanor was a prime target for such a fate. Worse was yet to come, though, for the rebel army threatened 'that the next day, they would place them in front of the storming party; and if the attacks were repelled, she and all the other ladies would be given up to the lowest ruffians in the camp'.

Christopher Aske related that, upon hearing of Lady Eleanor's perilous situation, and 'with the privity of none but the vicar of Skipton, a groom of the stables and a boy, he ... conveyed all the ladies into the castle' at night. One of the Clifford daughters amongst them was Lady Katherine, the mother of a future custodian of Mary Queen of Scots during her captivity at Bolton Castle. Katherine lived on till the age of eighty-five, over sixty years after her rescue.

A late 19th-century *Ballad of Christopher Aske* recalled this incident, but mixed up Eleanor's father-in-law and husband, as well as referring to her 'children', two of whom had not yet been born. The close kinship of the Aske brothers with the Cliffords came through their mother, Lady Elizabeth, who was the Shepherd Lord's sister. She was married into a junior branch of the Aske family before the Cliffords' fortunes were revived under the Tudors, and her home for the rest of her life was the small village of Aughton in East Yorkshire, a few miles away from her mother's ancestral home at Londesborough, where Lady Elizabeth spent her youth. The grey church tower at Aughton still bears a weather-beaten inscription which mentions Elizabeth's son Christopher, and the date 1536, for in addition to his exertions on the Cliffords' behalf that year, he paid for the tower of his home village church to be rebuilt.

Lady Eleanor had her two younger children – a daughter

named Margaret and another son, Charles – before she became the Countess of Cumberland in 1542. In Lady Anne Clifford's history of her ancestors, a family tradition was alluded to, concerning a rather bleak prediction made by the star-gazing Shepherd Lord about Eleanor's husband. His horoscope apparently indicated that he would father two sons, whose offspring would be embroiled in many lawsuits until the male line of descent died out. This foretold the situation of Lady Anne herself and her kinsmen in the next generation, however, instead of referring to Eleanor's sons. The deaths of both of them in infancy meant that their sister, Margaret, became the sole heiress of the Clifford inheritance, like Lady Anne after both her older brothers died. Another similarity between these Clifford daughters was that there seemed to be little prospect of further siblings for them – not due to marital breakdown with Lady Margaret's parents, as it was with Lady Anne's, but the health of her young mother Eleanor began to deteriorate.

Eleanor sent an affectionate, but urgent letter to her husband, addressing him as her 'dere hart' and requesting a physician, when she was taken seriously ill during a stay at the Clifford manor of Carleton, near Skipton. She thought she may be suffering from jaundice and an ague, because her urine was then 'very redd'. One of her other symptoms was severe pain in her side, which was reminiscent of a recurrent complaint later mentioned by Mary Queen of Scots during bouts of sickness. Historians have put forward the idea that Eleanor's illness may possibly have been the disease, porphyria, which has afflicted various members of the royal family through the ages, including the Queen of Scots and King George III.

An older half-sister of Eleanor's, Lady Anne Powys, was visiting her at the time she despatched her letter. This lady outlived her by several years, but Eleanor herself only outlived her Uncle Henry VIII by about ten months, when she died in November 1547, aged twenty-eight. Her daughter, Lady Margaret Clifford, was then seven years old and looked like the King's elder daughter, Mary, a resemblance which was to work both for and against her. She was almost orphaned during the immediate aftermath of losing her mother, when her father also fell ill. His life was saved in the nick of time, and the tale is told that part of his recovery involved sucking milk from a woman's breasts as his main sustenance!

When he had regained his health, the 2nd Earl of Cumberland looked towards one of the other great northern families, the Dacres, for a second wife who might give him a male heir. Eventually, the next Lady Anne arrived on the scene, even though the Cliffords and Dacres had long waged an ongoing feud. The tangled web of kinship meant that his intended bride was also his long-dead stepmother's niece. Anne Dacre was many years younger than the Earl, and she showed little enthusiasm for the match at first and kept him waiting until after he and all the Court attended his daughter's magnificent wedding at Whitehall Palace.

Lady Margaret Clifford married the Earl of Derby's eldest son Henry Stanley, Lord Strange, on 12 February 1555 – the first anniversary of the execution of her cousin, Lady Jane Grey, the nine-days' Queen. The nuptial ceremony and celebrations were as lavish as those of Margaret's parents. Her father shortly remarried at the far more remote setting of Kirkoswald Castle, a Dacre stronghold in Cumbria. The Earl and his new Countess then had five children in five years, but the first three were daughters, before at last the longed-for sons were born and given the names George and Francis.

The Countess was depicted in her granddaughter, Lady Anne Clifford's family memoir as a very domestic woman throughout her life and surprise was expressed that she never left the north of England. Despite this, however, she was still sometimes close to mainstream events of Tudor times. She may have visited the captive Mary Queen of Scots at Bolton Castle, for instance, due to the royal custodian there, Lord Scrope, being a Clifford nephew. And she also experienced the sadness of seeing members of her own immediate family, such as her brother, 'Crookback' Leonard

*Brass memorial in Skipton Church to Henry, Earl of
Cumberland and his 2nd wife, Anne, with their offspring,
including Lady Anne Clifford's father, George*

Dacre, rebel against Queen Elizabeth. His property was
forfeited to the Crown, a loss which was especially poignant
for her, as it included Kirkoswald Castle and happened a
few months after her husband died early in 1570. Later that
year, the widowed Countess Anne was mentioned during
the interrogation of a man called Henry Simpson, who had
been carrying messages between northern rebels. He
disclosed that when he visited her, she gave him forty
shillings for his travel expenses.

The Countess and her sister-in-law, Lady Katherine, were
amongst several leading Catholics in Yorkshire who earned
rebukes from the Archbishop of York for their religious
beliefs. When her son George arrived at Skipton Castle with
his bride, Margaret Russell, after their grand London
wedding, a culture clash prevailed all too soon – not only
was there a north-south divide but also one of different
faiths, as the new Countess Margaret of Cumberland came
from a strictly Protestant family.

Until her marriage, Margaret's only encounter with highland areas had been a visit to the Peak District and Buxton in the company of other Protestant ladies when she was fourteen. She made further visits to the healing well at Buxton from the draughty Clifford castles, for unfortunately her health suffered, amid her sense of isolation and neglect when she was a young wife left in unfamiliar surroundings with her mother-in-law. Her plight attracted sympathy from her royal sister-in-law, Margaret Clifford, who was by then the Countess of Derby and had also known unhappiness and ill-health, especially after her own marriage foundered, partly due to her husband's infidelity. Fully aware therefore of the problems besetting her younger namesake, Countess Margaret of Derby tried to remonstrate with both Earl George and his mother over improving his wife's quality of life.

The Countess of Derby had consulted faith-healers in an attempt to alleviate her own personal ailments. The Elizabethan antiquary, William Camden, wrote of her 'that through an idle mixture of curiosity and ambition ... she much used the conversations of necromancers and figure-flingers ...' This may have seemed like second nature to her, with the Clifford half of her ancestry including characters such as the Shepherd Lord and also her father, who had an extensive library on alchemy and chemistry, and dabbled in distilling waters for medicinal use. However, for a lady in line to the throne, such interests were viewed as deeply suspicious by Queen Elizabeth, and as Camden said, 'upon which account, she lost a share in the queen's inclinations'. Perhaps Margaret's family likeness to Queen Mary Tudor also antagonized Elizabeth and brought back unwelcome memories of the half-sister who had cast a perilous shadow over her own youth.

Even so, Margaret Clifford, Countess of Derby, and her cousin, Lady Catherine Grey, had the distinction of being the only members of the Tudor royal family to have more than one male offspring who reached mature adulthood. Two of her sons died in childhood, as did in her daughter, but Margaret herself lived until her niece and family biographer, Lady Anne Clifford, was six years old. After Margaret's intervention with Earl George on his wife's behalf, the marriage appeared to mend for a while, especially during the years following his mother, Countess Anne's death in 1581. For Countess Margaret of Cumberland, this was a time of better health, and with the births of three children and chances of contact with an increasing number of Protestants in the north, she came briefly into the nearest semblance of happiness she was ever to enjoy. She even succeeded in persuading Queen Elizabeth to allow the Earl to serve in the English fleet against the Spanish Armada in 1588, which suited him much more that the original royal command to join the army.

The energy shown by Earl George for his gambling and various expensive naval expeditions has been said to have passed on to his daughter, but found its more creative outlet with her in the restoration projects which brought her such renown. Lady Anne Clifford emphasized her resemblance to both her parents with autobiographical details such as: 'The colour of mine eyes was black, like my father's, and the form and aspect of them was quick and lively like my mother's. The hair of my head was brown and very thick, and so long that it reached to the calf of my legs when I stood upright, with a peak of hair on my forehead, and a dimple on my chin, and exquisite shape of body, like my father.' She declared that she was 'very happy' with her appearance in her youth and added: 'Though I say it, the perfections of my mind were much above those of my body. I had a strong and copious memory; a sound judgment and a discerning spirit; and so much of a strong imagination in me as at many times even my dreams and apprehensions proved to be true.' Contemporary descriptions of Lady Anne told of attributes such as her charitable nature, piety, fortitude, temperance in habits and care with finances, which all clearly came from her beloved and long-suffering mother.

Despite her father's frequent absences at Court, or else

Lady Anne's 'deare mother' Margaret, Countess of Cumberland

on voyages, Lady Anne enjoyed a happy childhood mostly under her mother's care. Members of Countess Margaret's family, including her aunt, Mrs Elmes of Lilford Hall, near Oundle in Northamptonshire, proved to be very supportive. During several lengthy visits to Lilford Hall, Anne 'was seasoned with ... love of a private country life, which ever continued in her'. Her education was entrusted to her governess, Mistress Taylor, and her tutor, Samuel Daniel, the poet who later wrote a Court masque called *Tethys' Festival*, in which Anne took part as a nymph of the river Aire, which flows by Skipton Castle.

The bond between mother and daughter strengthened further when Lady Anne was fifteen. Her father's extravagance over many years had placed great strain on the Clifford finances and inheritance long before he died in 1605, and in his will, he disposed of her property illegally. A royal writ of medieval times had stated that some of the Clifford lands were to pass from parent to offspring in the direct line of descent, including females. But Earl George bequeathed them instead to his brother, Francis, and so fulfilled the prediction of their great-grandfather, the Shepherd Lord, about family strife and litigation. The legal bids for Lady Anne to gain her inheritance became so bitter and acrimonious that her Uncle Francis Clifford ensured the gates of Skipton Castle were firmly shut against her and Countess Margaret.

Francis Clifford's youngest daughter, Lady Frances, married a cousin of that other Frances with Clifford blood, whose elopement had such an unforeseen impact on Earl George and his family – Frances Frecheville. As for Lady Anne, who lived until just over a century after that escapade, she never wavered in the belief she expressed on her father's epitaph in Skipton Church: 'he was the last heir male of the Cliffords that rightfully enjoyed those ancient lands in Westmoreland and in Craven' and she was his 'daughter and sole heir'. Anne had to wait *thirty-eight years* before she at last succeeded to her inheritance! She was then aged fifty-three and kept in mind that as both her parents died in middle age, she would have little time to enjoy this, after all those years of discord and traumas in pursuit of her lifelong quest.

Most of those years of waiting were also beset by marital difficulties. According to contemporary judges of character, her first husband, Richard Sackville, Earl of Dorset, was 'a licentious spendthrift, but a man of spirit and talent' and her second – Philip Herbert, Earl of Pembroke and Montgomery – was 'an ingrate, an ignoramus, a common swearer, a bully and a coward'. She lived mostly at Knole House in Kent during her first marriage and at Wilton House, Wiltshire, for part of her second. Although both marriages produced sons, none survived infancy, but she also had two daughters, Margaret and Isabel, by her first husband and she lived to see their children and some of their grandchildren. The elder daughter, Margaret, was named after Anne's own mother and was born two years before Countess Margaret died in 1616.

Lady Anne was at odds with her first husband because

of his attempts to raise money through her, so that he could fund his lavish lifestyle. She withstood all his persuasions to let go of her claim to the Clifford inheritance and accept ex gratia cash payments instead. The circumstances of her second marriage were even worse, and she wrote of how, in her unhappiness, she coped with 'good books and virtuous thoughts my companions, which can never discern affliction, nor be daunted when it unjustly happens; and by a happy genius I overcame all these troubles; the prayers of my blessed mother helping me therein'. She was separated from her husband for most of this marriage and was already back in the north, in full possession of her Clifford property, before she was widowed for a welcome second time.

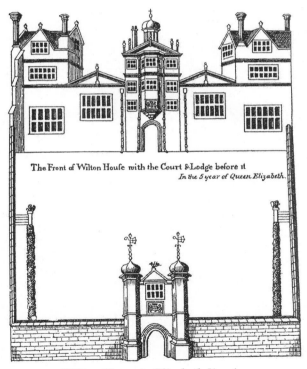

The Front of Wilton House with the Court & Lodge before it
In the 5 year of Queen Elizabeth.

Wilton House in Elizabeth I's reign

She made much use, however, of the noble title of Countess of Pembroke which she acquired from her second marriage, and also the initials 'A.P.' for Anne Pembroke on inscriptions recording her restoration work. One of the most poignant inscriptions is on the Countess Pillar near the main road to Penrith, in Cumbria, and on the very spot where she saw her mother for the last time: 'This Pillar was erected … by Anne, Countess Dowager of Pembroke … for a memorial of her last parting in this place with her good and pious mother, the Right Honourable Margaret, Countess Dowager of Cumberland, the 2nd of April, 1616. In memory whereof she also left an annuity of four pounds, to be distributed to the poor within the parish of Brougham every second day of April for ever, upon the stone table hereby.'

Keep of Appleby Castle, Cumbria

The love of country life, which Lady Anne Clifford developed during childhood, reached its full strength after her return to her great northern estates. She made the most of the 'contentments and innocent pleasures' of her new life for the thirty years which remained to her. She never went back south again, but journeyed much between Skipton and Brougham Castles along 'Lady Anne's Way'. Both of these were 'built up' under her supervision, as well as Barden Tower and the other Clifford castles at Appleby, Brough and Pendragon. She set up almshouses for a dozen poor widows, and restored churches, chapels, tombs and even a necessary bridge near the aptly-named Hell Gill in rough mountain terrain. Having been 'happy to be beloved in hir childhood by Queen Elizab.', Lady Anne became regarded almost as a queen in the north of England for many years. Her long and active life ended very peacefully at Brougham Castle in March 1676 and she was laid to rest in her table tomb beside that of her mother, in the Clifford Chapel at Appleby Church in Cumbria.

If only her 'bad father', Earl George, had realized that despite his grief at losing his young love, Gertrude Holles, he did far better than he knew by begetting his 'sole heir', Lady Anne.

Brougham Castle

CHAPTER 2

'Putt Out to Secular Habett'

A century before Lady Anne Clifford resided at Wilton House, another female writer is reputed to have recorded her own experiences of living and leaving there. Her name was Alice Langton and she was one of the thirty-three nuns of Wilton Abbey. A diary attributed to her was beautifully expressed in the way it evoked the atmosphere at the nunnery in 1539:

> *'March. I have ta'en a last look at the dear old home; and every room and cloistered walk did fill my mind with sweet and bitter memories, and vain regretfulness. I shall no more see the shadows of the cloister-arches stealing along the pavement, like figures in a dream, as I was wont to do, what time the summer sun rode high, and I did use to wear away the long bright hours in working at my 'broidery frame. I shall no more hear the soft sweet voice of Sister Willoughby uttering the 'Jube Domine' after refection in the Dining Hall ... I shall no more perform the offices of hospitality in the Guest-Hall, or make confession in the Chapter, or relieve the poor and needy at the Almonry, or pace the pleasant garden walks ... the while I watched the sleek-winged doves circling about their cote in sportive playfulness, heedful in no wise of the desolation which was falling on our House. It is all gone by; and the closing gate, which grated on its hinges as we passed, did also harshly grate upon my heart.'*

Alice Langton was one of four Wilton nuns who received an annual pension of £6, almost £1 more than the Sister Christian Willoughby mentioned in the diary. Alice 'took up her abode' in the neighbourhood of the abbey after it was closed, apparently for the rest of her life. She accepted the offer of a home with a former pupil, 'Lora Wodelande, the

A Benedictine nun

Reve's daughter of Ugford', near the village of Burcombe, who wished to 'requite … the pains I have bestowed on her instruction, though questionless it did not merit such return'. Lora probably had a relative who was mentioned on the Wilton pension list as 'Crystyan Wodelande', one of another four nuns awarded a pension of £5 each. But Lora's 'sisterly affection' towards Alice and thoughtful ways of welcome, such as the flowers she placed on the window ledge in the Alice's new room, 'did minister occasion for tranquil, and it may be, happy thoughts' to the former nun who woke up with a start on her first morning away from the nunnery. She had been dreaming about 'a mass for the repose of the soul of a departed sister' and then with 'much amaze, I looked about me at the unfamiliar aspect of my dormitory'. When she suddenly recalled the nuns' expulsion from Wilton Abbey and 'my coming hither yesterday, my heart grew heavy', but soon Lora tiptoed in so softly to see her that Alice 'blessed her for the home her love had opened to me in my exile and did resolve in years to come to manifest my thankfulness …'

Amongst the religious changes of the time, a law had already been passed in 1534, giving the King, instead of the Pope, supreme authority over the numerous abbeys and priories in his realm. But it was a royal 'commaundement' of 1538 which caused Alice Langton and all other ex-nuns in Tudor England to face another major difference to their daily lives – the question of what to wear! Under the new law, 'noe religious persons of the suppressed houses … should goe abroade in theyr religious habytes'. Nuns were to dress in the secular clothes of gentlewomen – in the words of the Windsor herald, Charles Wriothesley in his book, *A Chronicle of England during the Reigns of the Tudors*, these women were therefore 'putt out to secular habett' when their nunneries were closed.

In a novel called *The Nun* by Rene Bazin, a scene shows a group of early 20th-century French nuns changing from their distinctive religious apparel, or habit, which immediately set them apart from the secular world, into women's everyday clothes donated to them, after their convent was suddenly shut down. How wary and vulnerable they all felt on their emergence into the outside world in unfamiliar attire, which was ill-fitting with regard to their minds as well as their bodies. They no longer had the sense of protection, which the wearing of their nuns' habits had given them, and they dared not even carry the rosary beads which usually hung from their waist, ready for use at any time.

Each different religious order had its own particular style of habit, and rules which determined the communal daily round of prayers and worship, work, study and hospitality and alms-giving. Most English nunneries, including Wilton Abbey, belonged to the Benedictine order, which followed the Rule of St Benedict. The members of these communities were known as 'Black Nuns, the most ancient of all the religious orders in this country' and so called because of 'their habits, a black robe with a scapulary of the same, and under that a tunic of white or undyed wool'. Other orders of nuns had names such as Cistercian, Augustinian, Gilbertine, Minoresses, Dominican, Cluniac and Bridgettine. A centuries-old way of life came to an end with the suppression of all religious houses by Henry VIII in the 1530s – the process well-known in history as the Dissolution of the Monasteries. For the nunneries, this struck a hard, double blow to their role in female education, both for the nuns' work as women teachers and for their pupils, often local girls and young women, whose nearby place of learning disappeared. Women teachers remained few in number for the rest of the Tudor period.

During the dynasty's early years, however, young women of noble and even royal rank were convent-educated. England's only Dominican nunnery at Dartford Priory in Kent, for instance, received Queen Elizabeth of York's ten year old sister, Princess Bridget, as a pupil in 1492. The Queen paid for her maintenance there, and Bridget seems to have had frequent family visits, as money payments were recorded 'for the cost of riding from Windsore to Dartford to my Lady Brigget by the space of too day at twelve pence a day'. When her mother, the Dowager Queen, Elizabeth Woodville, fell dangerously ill in 1493, Bridget was allowed to visit her in the royal apartments at Bermondsey Abbey, south London, where she had previously retired. The Dowager Queen died there, 'in the arms of her daughters, all of whom were present at the mournful scene, with the exception of the Queen, who was precluded by her approaching accouchement' with her fourth child.

The other three daughters were Princesses Cecily, Catherine and Anne. Bridget was also with them to attend their mother's funeral at Windsor Castle, where she was buried beside their father, Edward IV. After returning by water to Dartford Priory, Bridget eventually 'took the veil' as a nun there, a ceremony which was marked with appropriate pomp for a royal lady and was well-attended by her family and the area's nobility and gentry. Some accounts relate that she became Prioress of Dartford, but throughout her years there, the nunnery was in fact ruled by the same Prioress, Elizabeth Cressener, who was in office from the late 1480s until her death in 1537. Bridget herself died in 1517 and was buried in the priory church.

The name 'Elizabeth Cressener' reappeared at the front of the pension list when the priory was dissolved in 1539. This nun was believed to be a niece of the late prioress, and because Dartford then became a royal Tudor residence, she very briefly continued a family tradition as prioress, when Queen Mary Tudor reinstated the nuns there during her reign. After Elizabeth I succeeded to the throne, however, she soon expelled them again.

At the great abbey of Shaftesbury in Dorset, two nuns whose names were on the pension list had also been connected with people in high places, but in very contrasting ways. As long ago as 1483, King Richard III had used a royal prerogative to present a young girl there at the time of his coronation: Elizabeth Bryther was therefore placed in the care of the Abbess, Margaret St John, the niece of Lady Margaret Beaufort, two years before this lady's

Tudor son, became King Henry VII. When the Dissolution occurred a mere fifty-four years later, Elizabeth Bryther was still at Shaftesbury, but she was amongst three nuns who were noted to be sick and lame then – one of them, Joan Amys, had also been a nun there since the late 15th century. A much younger nun, 'Dorothy Clansy' or Clausey, whose name was further down the pension list, provided an example of how nunneries were sometimes used as convenient dumping grounds for illegitimate daughters. Her father was for long the most powerful churchman and statesman in the land – Cardinal Wolsey. His attempt at a cover-up, regarding paternity of her, was only divulged after his death, when a hapless official called 'John Clusey' wrote that Wolsey had 'caused' him to put her 'to the nunnery of Shaftesbury and there to be professed, and would have her to be named my daughter, and the truth is she was his daughter'. He mentioned too that fourteen year old Dorothy then wanted to leave Shaftesbury Abbey, but he preferred her to stay there and become a nun, which she clearly did. Yet she still gained her first wish when she reached her early twenties – and with a fairly generous annual pension of £4, which was as much as some prioresses of small nunneries received.

The precedents for suppression were established long before the full-scale Dissolution. Usually, closures were carried out so that the revenues of a religious house could be diverted for male religious or educational purposes, such as the founding of colleges. In 1497, the nunnery of St Radegund in Cambridge was suppressed by Henry VII, partly because of the 'ill lives of the nuns, being occasioned by the nearness of the University'. Its building and income were re-used for the newly-established Jesus College.

Another Cambridge college, St John's, founded under Lady Margaret Beaufort's will, received an extra endowment in 1522 from a former Kent nunnery in the diocese of her executor, John Fisher, Bishop of Rochester. Lillechurch Priory was reported to be a gathering place for 'lewd persons' and so the nuns there had achieved notoriety for their immoral lives. They had been without a prioress since 1520 and only three nuns remained there. The Vicar of Higham in Kent had fathered children by two of them. The witnesses who informed Bishop Fisher about them included a nurse, who had taken on the responsibility of caring for one nun's child, and a former Lillechurch servant, who encountered this nun weeping in the cloisters one day, bemoaning her bad luck that she had been unable to keep 'this thynge ... unknowen and hydden'.

Cardinal Wolsey also dabbled in suppressions, to raise funds for his own college-founding schemes at Oxford and Ipswich. Amongst the twenty or so priories he caused to be dissolved before 1525, an extreme example of scandal occurred at the Benedictine nunnery of Littlemore, a few miles south of Oxford. The naughtiest of its nuns was the Prioress, Katherine Wells, who had borne an illegitimate daughter to a Kentish priest and she set aside household utensils, beds and linen belonging to the priory, to provide a dowry for her child. Although the girl died, the parents continued their liaison. Any complaints from the five nuns under this Prioress about her sinful life were severely punished by her, with physical violence and putting them in the stocks. On one occasion, three nuns broke these while rescuing one of their sisters, and then burnt the dreaded stocks. The four nuns also broke a window and escaped through it, away from the Prioress's wrath. They did not dare to return to the priory for several weeks. The Prioress, in her turn, accused them of more bad behaviour, such as amusing themselves during church services and, in the case of one nun, of following her own example by bearing a child, whose father was a local married man.

More complaints and tale-telling emerged, however, about Wolsey's servants and the unscrupulous methods they used in closing down priories in various counties, especially mentioning a ruthlessly efficient man called Thomas Cromwell. His work for Wolsey was paving the way for the future, though, for he had observed how vulnerable the religious houses would be if they were faced with the all-out onslaught which eventually came after he entered the royal service. And then, he no longer supervised suppressions to raise funding for colleges, but to refill the depleted treasury of the extravagant King.

During the decade before Wilton Abbey added its large annual revenue to Henry VIII's coffers, it too suffered 'enormities' amongst its nuns, in addition to an outbreak of plague, a fire which destroyed their dormitory and much wrangling and political interference over the choice of a new abbess, after the old one, Dame Cecily Willoughby, died in 1528. The King was then so besotted with Anne Boleyn that he was minded to grant her wishes over any matter. Anne's brother-in-law, William Carey, had made a dying request to her that she would have his sister Eleanor, a nun at Wilton, to be appointed as abbess. In the meantime, though, Wolsey had decided to support the existing Prioress there, Isabel Jordan. Both candidates had broken their nuns' vow of chastity in the past, but Eleanor Carey had also borne two illegitimate children to a priest and followed these misdemeanours with an affair with a nobleman's servant! Even King Henry baulked at agreeing to this particular request from Anne, and Wolsey ensured that the Wilton nuns elected his choice as abbess.

By 1533, the position again fell vacant after the death of Isabel Jordan. In the nun's diary of Alice Langton was a rare, sour note when she wrote of the last 'Lady Abbess', Cecily Bodenham, soon before the Dissolution: 'Methinks the Abbess hath a faint heart and doth yield up our possessions to the Spoiler with a not unwilling haste, concerning which, Master Richard Nevill, the Sub-Seneschal informeth me His Majesty's Commissioners do purpose to reward her with a fair house at Foffount, and a goodly stipend withal.'

Four years earlier, Cecily Bodenham had borrowed money to make certain that the political manoeuvring over her election as Abbess of Wilton went in her favour. If she had stayed in her former position as Prioress of the small Wiltshire nunnery of Kington St Michael, she would have received an annual pension of £5 after its suppression. But

*A Tudor abbess with her symbol of office, the crozier:
brass memorial to Dame Elizabeth Hervey (1527) in
Elstow Abbey Church, Bedfordshire*

her move to Wilton Abbey raised her to the rank of a peeress of the realm, and brought her a suitable settlement accordingly at the Dissolution, as the pension list reveals: 'Cecily Bodenham, abbess, £100 and the house of Foffounte [Fovant] with the orchards, gardens and three acres of meadow and pasture belonging to the same, and also every week one load of wood to be taken out of the King's wood of Foffounte by the appointment of the King's officers'.

Conditions at her previous priory were probably so poor that they may have reflected those at the one remaining nunnery in Staffordshire, the Blackladies Priory at Brewood, near Wolverhampton, where Prioress Isabel Launder even had to share a bed with one of her three nuns. The last Prioress of Kington St Michael was Mary Denys, described as 'a faire yong woman of Laycok' (Lacock Abbey, also in Wiltshire), and she obtained the £5 pension and went to live in Bristol when her priory was dissolved in 1536.

Mary's predecessor, Dame Cecily, had indeed come a long way from the time when she herself, as a young prioress, was abducted in 1511 by a curate from the picturesque village of Castle Combe after he robbed her priory! With the grand lifestyle of a great lady which Cecily Bodenham attained in her retirement, there seems little likelihood that she would have accepted returning to Wilton Abbey, as told in a colourful story which appeared in *Brief Lives* by John Aubrey in the 17th century: 'In Queen Mary's time, upon the return of the Catholic religion, the nuns came again to Wilton Abbey, and this William, Earl of Pembroke [the new owner] with his cap in hand, fell upon his knee to the lady abbess and the nuns ... Upon Queen Mary's death, the earl came to Wilton (like a tiger) and turned them out, crying, "Out, ye whores, to work, to work, ye whores, go spin".'

The smaller priories were those with an income of less than £200 a year and the Suppression Act passed by Parliament in 1536 offered pensions only to the head of each dissolved priory. Other members of these former communities had the option of transferring to a larger establishment of the same religious order. Some of the nuns from Cannington Priory in Somerset, for instance, found a new home at Shaftesbury Abbey. At the 'Priory of Nuns' of Thetford in Norfolk, however, 'all except the prioress', the elderly Dame Elizabeth Hothe, 'sought release' from their nuns' vows.

Legbourne nunnery, near Louth, Lincolnshire, was in the very process of being dissolved in early October 1536, when the Lincolnshire Rebellion (mentioned in Chapter 1) broke out at Louth and armed rebels led by a local shoemaker marched to Legbourne and seized the commissioners at work there. The Prioress, Jane Messendyne, and 'systers of the pryory of Legborne' had hoped that their 'poor priory … may be preserved', as they said in a submissive letter appealing to Thomas Cromwell earlier in the year, and that despite closures elsewhere 'because of theire myslyving … ye shall here no complayntes against us nother in our lyvyng nor hospitalitie keepyng'.

The wording of the Suppression Act denounced all the small religious houses as dens of 'abominable living' and extolled the larger abbeys as if they were peopled by paragons of virtue, who 'right well kept and observed' religion. In reality, though, there were good, devout paragons and naughty nuns in convents large and small. One of the sauciest alleged incidents, for instance, was attributed to one of the largest nunneries, Syon Abbey in Middlesex. An unnamed nun there was propositioned to break her vow of chastity – with her own confessor. 'He persuaded her … making her to believe that whensoever and as oft as they should meddle together, if she were immediately afterwards confessed by him and took of him absolution, she should be clear forgiven of God …'

And despite such reports, life continued at the larger houses, while the occupants of smaller ones faced surrender of a different kind – that of their very place of residence. Remote Catesby Priory, near the western boundary of Northamptonshire, and Polesworth Abbey, in neighbouring Warwickshire, both received very favourable pre-

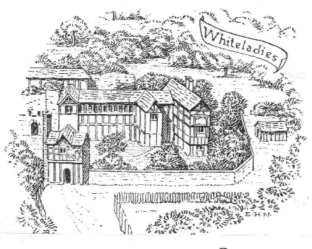

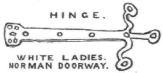

Before and after the Dissolution: the Augustinian nunnery of Whiteladies, Brewood, Shropshire

Dissolution reports from the royal commissioners. The report on Catesby in May 1536 'found the house in very perfect order ... as good as we have ever seen ... If any religious house is to stand, none is more meet ... than Catesby'. Henry VIII suspected that his officials had 'received rewards' from the nuns to write this.

Polesworth was also recommended to 'remayne unsuppressed'. The Abbess, Dame Alice FitzHerbert, was a 'discreet and religious woman' like the Prioress of Catesby, Joyce Bekeley, and both had held office for over twenty-five years. The twelve 'vertuous and religious nonnes' of Polesworth would 'never one ... leave nor forsake their habite'. An extra consideration concerning this 'nonnery' was the dependence of the local people on it – if it were dissolved, 'the towne will shortly after fall to ruin and decay' and the people would then have 'to seke for their lyving'.

Abbess Alice was permitted to buy exemption from suppression for Polesworth, which continued its seven centuries of existence for another three years. Prioress Joyce of Catesby also offered to pay for her priory to continue and made a direct plea to the new Queen, Jane Seymour, for help. She wrote a heartfelt letter to Thomas Cromwell, asking him to 'second the Queen's efforts', and detailing some of her own efforts, such as offering the King '2,000 marks for the house of Catisby'. As there had not yet been 'a perfect answer', she added, 'I beg you, in my great sorrow, get the King to grant that the house may stand ... You shall have 100 marks of me to buy a gelding, and my prayers during my life, and all my sisters during their lives ...'

Sadly for her and the nine nuns of Catesby, the answer was far from perfect – the commissioner, George Giffard, who had praised this priory so highly, was sent to suppress it later in 1536. When Queen Jane made a gentle intercession with the King to keep Catesby and other religious houses open, she bore in mind her personal motto, 'Bound to obey and serve'. She knelt before the King to plead with him, but even this deferential approach incurred his increasingly terrifying anger and led to the only recorded disagreement to mar the usual tranquility of his third marriage. Jane was curtly ordered to get up from her knees, then told off and given a salutary reminder that her predecessor, Queen Anne Boleyn, had died for interfering in state matters! Jane took his warning to heart, realizing that she was powerless to help the dissolved religious houses, despite her personal sympathy for them. She subsequently followed the safer option of concentrating on domestic matters.

Two of Queen Jane's cousins, Katherine and Jane Wadham, were nuns at the ancient and wealthy Romsey Abbey in Hampshire. Katherine was appointed sub-prioress in 1536, though she had been professed as a nun only two years beforehand, at the age of twenty-three. Two of the eight other young women, Marion Goddard and Katherine Woodward, professed with Katherine at the same ceremony in Romsey's magnificent Abbey Church, were only fourteen years old. The oldest new nun was Agnes Hall, aged thirty-one. Katherine's sister, Jane, was the sextoness of Romsey and had already been there for several years – she later said that she had been 'forced by threats … to become a nun'.

A previous holder of both offices of sub-prioress and sextoness had been deprived of her positions of responsibility for negligence and carelessness. Clemence Malyn confessed to unauthorized meetings with a priest in different parts of the church, even leaving a key to a part known as 'paradise' in a hole near the door, so that he could let himself into the building. She denied any wrongdoing between them, yet lied to the Abbess, Elizabeth Ryprose, who thought there was a thief in the church one evening when he entered there after curfew, and Dame Clemence told her that the church was empty.

Another naughty nun of Romsey, who was punished partly by demotion in the nunnery was called Anne Talke. Her offences were unspecified in the abbey records, but they were considered serious enough to earn her the penance of a month's imprisonment and a fast on Saturdays, when she could have 'bread and water only'. Perhaps her transgressions included the grim pun on her surname, 'Talke', of which other nuns certainly were guilty. Alice Gorsyn, for example, clearly found her nerves frayed by a constant daily existence cooped up in an all-female environment and she confessed to verbally abusing other nuns, and criticizing and spreading bad tales about them behind their backs. She was sentenced to be excommunicated, but later absolved from this rather drastic fate. Alice Gorsyn was given a penance instead, that if she succumbed to her old conduct in future, a tongue made of red cloth was to be attached to the item of apparel called the barbe, which the nuns wore under the chin, and to shame her by being on display there for a month! This punishment was to be repeated each time she re-offended.

The infamous diet of bread and water was inflicted on a Romsey nun called Margaret Dowman, on every third and sixth day for a whole year of imprisonment after she admitted 'misconduct' with 'one Thomas Hordes'. On those bread and water days, she was also to be further punished with 'discipline' during the daily meetings in the chapter-house. Amongst other indignities was the curious requirement that any candle she might carry in a procession had to be borne with the point facing downwards.

A coincidence occurred in two other Benedictine nunneries, which were at opposite ends of the country: at Malling Abbey in Kent, the Abbess, Elizabeth Rede shared her name with two of the six nuns at the lonely priory of Holystone in the Cheviot Hills of Northumberland. The pair at Holystone were distinguished by local place-names, 'alias Morpeth' and 'alias Redesdale', and there was also an Agnes Rede amongst the other four nuns. Life for these northern nuns would have been very frugal and devoid of comfort, compared with that for the southern Elizabeth Rede, whose father was a leading Tudor judge. But she did suffer some discomfort, in the form of emotional distress, when she found herself in deep trouble with Thomas Cromwell, by trying to appoint one of her own kinsmen as steward of Malling Abbey and refusing Cromwell's nomination of his nephew for this office.

Sometimes, as shown in Alice Langton's diary at Wilton Abbey, the former head of a priory moved to take charge at a larger nunnery for worldly gain in terms of prestige and affluence. Unlike Wilton, however, where the last abbess filled an already vacant position, the situation at Malling was an ominous development for the wealthier religious houses. Elizabeth Rede resigned as Abbess and was replaced by a very pliable friend of Cromwell's, called Margaret Vernon. She had been governess to his son and had recently 'shown herself a wise woman' as Prioress of Little Marlow, Buckinghamshire, by readily surrendering it, 'glad with all my hart', as she wrote to Cromwell and trusting, with regard to her future, that she would have 'necessity neither to begge nor to fall to ... other unconvenyence'. There was little danger of begging – her pension payout increased tenfold after she became the last Abbess of Malling and surrendered that nunnery too, in 1539.

Early in her tenure at Malling, Margaret Vernon was approached to accommodate her downhearted predecessor. The matter was raised on Elizabeth Rede's behalf by her brother-in-law in a letter to Cromwell, in which she 'humbly' beseeched that she could have 'that room and lodging' in the Abbey which previous abbesses 'that hath likewise resigned used to have' and 'such plate' which she had been given by her father to be returned to her.

The heads of larger abbeys probably began to realize that the days were numbered for their houses too, after the collapse of the Lincolnshire and Pilgrimage of Grace rebellions in 1536-7. These led to the suppression of great northern abbeys such as Jervaulx in Yorkshire, which had been targeted by the rebels to involve the monks. The King's actions in re-founding a Lincolnshire nunnery at Stixwould, previously a priory for white-robed nuns of the Cistercian order, may not have been enough to reassure worried abbesses and prioresses elsewhere. The Cistercian nuns of Stixwould had received £1 each when their priory was dissolved in 1536. Its revival became necessary when a community of Benedictine nuns were re-located from the county's Stainfield Priory, which had obtained exemption from suppression. The new prioress, Mary Missenden, also had two other family members amongst her nuns. Henry VIII ordered Cromwell to witness the charter of Stixwould, which stated that this nunnery was 'to last for ever'. It was placed under the rule of a strict, white-habited order known as Premonstratensian, but a little over two years after its founding, Prioress Mary was required to surrender Stixwould, during an intensive time of suppressions.

Cromwell's post-bag of letters from women included several missives from an abbess whose election he supported at Godstow Abbey, Oxfordshire, in 1535. Katherine Bulkeley 'alias' Bewmarys' came from a Cheshire family, whose connections with North Wales were in the very heartland of the Tudors' early ancestry on the Isle of Anglesey. Her eldest brother, Sir Richard Bulkeley, was then Constable of Beaumaris Castle. She aimed to keep Thomas Cromwell's favour by writing to him words such as, 'Of your mere goodness you have brought me of nothing to all I have'. She sent him gifts such as Banbury cheeses and offered him the stewardship of Godstow with '20 or 30 men to do the King's service', which she thanked him that 'he was good enough to accept'.

Godstow Abbey had merited a favourable report in the year she became its Abbess. As befitted its position on the banks of the river Isis, north of the nearby university at Oxford, the nunnery had a high reputation for its education of young gentlewomen from the surrounding area, and many appeals were made to the King to save it, so that it could continue its educational work. The Abbess's letters remained courteous towards Cromwell himself, but from November 1538, their tone turned bitter when complaining about her 'mortal enemye' who arrived suddenly that month 'with a great rout upon him, and dothe threaten me and my sisters, saying he hathe the King's commission to suppress the house'.

This official was called Dr John London, who described her as receiving him 'pensively'. He had opposed Abbess

Katherine's election and she was sure he 'had ever since borne great malice' towards her – she may have judged his character correctly, for he was later convicted of perjury over another matter. When she refused to surrender Godstow Abbey to him, he resorted to intimidation of the nuns 'one by one' and herself by denouncing her to Cromwell as a 'spoiler and waster'. She defended herself against such an accusation, saying that 'the contrary is true, for I have not alienated one halporthe of goods ... but have rather increased the same'. A further gripe was the length and cost of Dr London's uninvited stay, but Cromwell soon earned her thanks for removing him from Godstow. She told Cromwell that she did 'not mean to surrender her house except at the King's command or his', and also assured him that the nuns rejected Catholic beliefs in 'Pope, Purgatory, image, pilgrimage and praying to dead saints' and had little enthusiasm for wearing their religious habits. They were all 'putt out to secular habett' with pensions a year later, but the voluntary surrender was overseen by another commissioner, Sir John Williams.

Perhaps one of the fifteen Godstow nuns, Mary Fiennes, returned to her family's splendid ancestral home at Broughton Castle in north Oxfordshire, where she would

Ruins of the Abbess's Chapel, Godstow Abbey, Oxfordshire

have been much nearer to Banbury and its cheeses than she was at Godstow! Her former abbess, Dame Katherine, returned to Cheshire, with a £50 annual pension, and lived near other members of the Bulkeley family. At Cheadle, her brother John was the absentee rector and she leased from him the parsonage, which became her new home. An inscription on a stained glass window once in Cheadle Church credited her with building the chancel there in 1556 and having 'all the windows glazed'. She was buried in the chancel three years later. Amongst the bequests in her will was 'a golde ringe with a blewe and a red stonne in the same', which she left to her niece with the touching message, 'desiringe her to accept the same for a simple token and remembrance, and to pray for me'. The recipient of Dame Katherine's best tablecloth, best towel and best carpet, however, was her nephew.

An ex-abbess whose retirement home must have been very comfortable, being filled with numerous cushions she embroidered herself, was Margaret Russell of Tarrant Abbey in Dorset. Her will mentioned 'three of my every day cushions and three of my holy day cushions' as well as a further 'two covered with sarcanet, one with green velvet wrought with gold and the other three wrought upon cloth with needlework'. She also embroidered 'one coverlet of white wrought with red and green branches' and 'a red coverlet with roses'. Various valuables included household items and pieces of jewellery, and her stylish, opulent clothes showed how well she adapted to 'secular habett': 'my best gown of silk chamlett, my kirtle of satin, my scarlet petticoat and my best bonnet of velvet ... my second best gown of grogoame ... and my kirtle of silk chamlet'.

In 1568, Dame Margaret was buried in the traditional resting-place for abbesses and nuns of Tarrant, in the Dorset church at Bere Regis. Part of the manor there, which had belonged to the abbey was acquired by the local gentry family, the Turbervilles, whose name was used in a different version by Thomas Hardy in his novel, *Tess of the D'Urbevilles*.

The will of an ex-abbess called Morphita Kingsmill, from Wherwell Abbey in the neighbouring county of Hampshire, revealed that when she died a year after Margaret Russell, she seemed to own many feather beds, bolsters, sheets, blankets, pillows and coverlets, which were all left to female beneficiaries. However, when the names of seven of these ladies – Elizabeth Pickering, Joan Woodlock, Morphita Vine, Joan Mate, Joan Dolling, Elizabeth Foster and Elizabeth Hacker 'now Edmond Bathe's wife' – are matched with the pension list for Wherwell, a picture emerges that six of Morphita Kingsmill's former nuns still dwelt with her. Elizabeth Hacker, whose husband was listed as one of the witnesses to the will, probably lived nearby. The will is believed to provide evidence that these former nuns continued with their communal religious life after the Dissolution of the Monasteries, possibly in a larger group in the early years after this, for the Wherwell pension list then numbered twenty-five.

Hampshire's oldest nunnery, St Mary's Abbey, Winchester, known as the Nuns' Minster or Nunnaminster, had a similar number of nuns in 1536. Its total establishment was found to consist of over a hundred people, though, with lay sisters, officials, priests, servants and about twenty-six children boarding there as pupils. Dame Elizabeth Shelley became Abbess in 1527 and one of the nuns was her niece, Margaret. Her brother, Sir William Shelley, lived about twelve miles from Winchester, but of greater potential significance for her and the Nunnaminster was that he was in favour with the King and this might be of use if she ever needed help. She had her own household and a 'gentyllwoman' companion called Jane Shirley. Other senior nuns in the abbey also had their own servants, including the sextoness, Margaret Leigh, whose brother Thomas worked as one of the Nunnaminster officials, and sub-prioress, Agnes Badgecroft, who was one of several nuns to continue as a small religious community in Winchester after the Dissolution.

Unusually, glimpses of the ongoing contact between these

ex-nuns came not from their former Abbess's will, but from those of three nuns whose names appeared on the pension list. Their bequests, or bequests made to them, further remembered four other of their 'sisters'. Elizabeth Shelley died in 1547, leaving money, clothing, jewellery and household goods to Agnes Badgecroft, Margaret Selwood, Maude Aldridge and niece Margaret Shelley, who received her aunt's 'best frock'. These ladies benefited too from the wills of Edburga Stratford and Joan Wayte, and Joan's brother was given most of a money bequest she herself had had from her deceased 'sister', Jane or Joan Gaynsford. When Dame Agnes Badgecroft died in 1556, the only surviving sister to benefit from her will was Margaret Shelley.

The pension list for Shaftesbury Abbey in 1539 included two of its fifty or more nuns as 'Marg. Mewe' and 'Edith Magdelan', whose names reappeared in an Elizabethan document over twenty years later as 'Margaret Mayo' and 'Edith Maudlen'. They settled in Shaftesbury after the Dissolution and rented two tenements near the abbey cemetery. Although there is no record of other ex-nuns sharing their house, informal arrangements may have been made, for instance, in continuing to care for the 'sick and lame' Elizabeth Bryther and Joan Amys (mentioned earlier in this chapter) and fellow-sufferer, Elizabeth Jakes. Another nun, Anne Bodenham, was a kinswoman of Abbess Cecily Bodenham of Wilton, whose new residence at Fovant was only a few miles across into neighbouring Wiltshire from Shaftesbury. Dame Cecily was known to have no close male relatives still alive – if Anne was in a similar situation, there is a possibility that she joined the ten former Wilton nuns in the household of her female relative at Fovant.

The last Abbess of Shaftesbury, Elizabeth Zouche, seems to have kept in touch with her former nuns. She gave pensions to them from her own income, her pension being even larger than that of Cecily Bodenham. Both Shaftesbury and Wilton, the two wealthiest nunneries in England, were dissolved on the same day in 1539, the Feast of the

Annunciation of the Blessed Virgin Mary – 25th March – known as Lady-Day in bygone times. Yet there was no hint at Shaftesbury of the collusion which Alice Langton's diary described regarding Wilton, between 'the Lady Abbess' who 'warned us surrender must be made to the King, His Majesty' and the royal commissioners who carried out the suppression.

Shaftesbury's Abbess Elizabeth Zouche had been in office by then for ten years and she refused to resign when one of her Wiltshire tenants, Sir Thomas Arundell, pressurized her to do so. She offered money instead, to both the King and Thomas Cromwell, to allow Shaftesbury Abbey to stay in existence. Their response was to offer money to her and the Shaftesbury nuns, in the form of pensions, but the wording of the deed of surrender for the abbey was somewhat in denial of the truth in stating that its hand-over to Henry VIII was done 'willingly and voluntarily'. The abbey buildings, including its cathedral-sized church, were totally demolished by order of the new secular owner – none other than Sir Thomas Arundell – apparently before he was executed for treason in 1552.

Various versions of house-sharing, whether with other ex-nuns, with their own families or friends, or for some former nuns – with husbands, were probably an essential part of life in the secular world for most of the 1,500 women 'putt out' of their nunneries to face the challenging, sometimes distressing process of re-adjustment. With little chance of finding gainful employment, their options were limited to mainly unrecorded domestic environments, whereas Tudor historical documents have detailed the fortunes of many ex-monks and canons who began new careers after the Dissolution. Neasham Priory in County Durham bucked the trend, for the last Prioress, Joan Lawson, was not 'putt out' at all, but went on living there for the remaining seventeen years of her life. She succeeded in a new career and also stayed in touch with the nine nuns formerly under her charge, one of whom had even been a naughty nun named 'Trowlope' or 'Trollop'!

Joan Lawson became involved in something of a local family enterprise in County Durham, which resulted in her and a prioress kinswoman, Agnes Lawson, of St Bartholomew's nunnery in Newcastle-upon-Tyne, working as lady farmers at opposite ends of the county after the Dissolution. Joan was near the river Tees in the south and Agnes's farm was near the river Tyne in the north. Joan Lawson was certainly well-connected, as her close and alive male relative, her brother James, was a Newcastle merchant. When her Teesside nunnery at Neasham was exempted from closure in 1537, she granted a lease of it to her brother. He became the new owner of the priory after it was finally suppressed in 1540, and she then rented it from him. Her life as a tenant farmer there included rearing livestock, as well as growing crops.

Agnes Lawson was also a livestock farmer, who kept cattle and sheep. She lived at Gateshead for twenty-six years after her Tyneside nunnery was dissolved in 1540. During her time as prioress there, she and her nuns let a farm at Gateshead to James Lawson. Her appointment in 1523 had been the occasion of some wrangling between Cardinal Wolsey and the abbot of Newminster Abbey in Northumberland, over whose right it was to decide on the successor to the recently deceased Prioress Joan Baxter. The abbot of Newminster first promoted Dame Agnes to the honour, but Wolsey declared this procedure invalid. 'The new elect prioress' then became the focus of some wry advice from Abbot Huby of Fountains Abbey in Yorkshire, who averred that for his sixty years as a monk, the nuns of St Bartholomew's had been 'under the jurisdiction of Newminster' and 'Dame Joan Baxter was created prioress' by the abbot. Huby thought 'it not worthwhile, however, to strive with the Cardinal but suffer the nuns of Newcastle to trip and dance in the same trace that all other their sisters have done'.

Perhaps this is the earliest written use of the term 'trip' to mean a light and nimble dance step – the word appeared in the 17th century in the work of William Shakespeare and

John Milton, though not in connection with nuns! Abbot Huby added that he had heard 'a good account of the young sister elect, and would not have her removed'. And neither did her sister-nuns, whether they danced or not, for after their second election in her favour, Agnes Lawson was reinstated as their Prioress.

In 1538, one of London's ex-nuns managed to net an abbot as her husband. As Charles Wriosthesley's *Chronicle* reported: 'The Abbot of Warden', Bedfordshire, 'maryed one which was a nonne at the Mineries, called Mistris Bures, and had continued there in religion above sixteen yeares'. The nearest equivalent name to 'Bures' on the pension list for 'the Minories, without Aldgate' nunnery is that of 'Margaret Boroughe'.

Unfortunately for them, though, a law was passed in the next year, which a contemporary observer summed up as follows: 'Priests and religious persons are forbidden to marry under pain of death. Those already married must separate from their wives and never to be taken in their company on pain of death. Vows of religious women are to be observed and transgressors to be judged as felons'. This was not repealed until early in 1548, a year after Henry VIII's death.

Some nuns, such as all nine of those at Blackburgh Priory in Norfolk, were known 'to have their dispensations' which freed them from two of their religious vows – poverty and obedience. But if the vow of chastity was forsaken for married life, this was frowned upon as incest if the wife had once been a nun. Elizabeth Hayward, a former Cluniac nun of Delapre Abbey in Northampton, was charged with committing this offence with a Bedfordshire gentleman from the village of Wymington. She was sentenced to do public penance, even though the 'gentleman' was her husband.

Wilton Abbey once housed a potential victim of this severe law. Her married name was Radegund Adelam, and her husband George, believing that she was a former Wilton nun, tried to end their marriage, using the provisions of this law as his chance to be free of her. Their divorce case in December 1541 included a witness called Christian Gardiner of Shoreham in Kent, who testified that she had known Radegund for twenty years. Mistress Gardiner recalled her as Radegund Delyngton 'waiting upon one Dame Agnes Pawsey, a nun of the same house'. Like Radegund, Dame Agnes was not mentioned on the pension list for Wilton, but she may have died between the time of Radegund serving her in the early 1520s and the abbey's demise in 1539. The name, 'Anne Dauncy', who received a pension of £4 and herself later married, has been suggested as being the mysterious Dame Agnes.

Christian Gardiner added that during a visit by the Bishop of Salisbury to Wilton, she saw Radegund amongst the nuns in their chapter house and when they came out, 'the said Radegunde did wear a white vayle'. The witness, 'being a secular' herself, 'did not go into the chapter house at that time', so she could not tell if Radegund had made 'any profession or solemn vow' before the Bishop. She pointed out, though, that 'they that was professed did wear a different manner of raiment than the said Radegunde did wear' and despite noticing Radegund with the black-veiled nuns 'at divine service time and in other places conversant with them', the future wife of George Adelam 'was not taken for one of those professed' and 'suddenly was gone, but where she went she cannot tell'. Novice Benedictine nuns wear a white veil during their preparatory training, so Radegund may have begun her novitiate at the time described by Christian Gardiner and her swift departure from the nunnery was a sign that a religious life was not, after all, for her.

George Adelam asked for the divorce case to be adjourned till a later date, but faced with the fact that his wife had not been fully professed as a nun, he did not even turn up to the re-scheduled hearing. Although the reason for his failure to appear was not given, it was probably due to a resigned acceptance by him that the chances of divorcing Radegund were very slender, under the circumstances.

In June 1541, six months before this attempted divorce case, a commission of enquiry was set up concerning the marriage of a nun and priest, who were both connected with

Romsey Abbey. The commission was directed 'to pronounce the marriage valid, if they shall so find it'. Queen Jane Seymour's cousin, the reluctant Romsey nun, Jane Wadham (mentioned earlier in this chapter), told the commission her chequered life story in a petition. She said that 'threats and machinations of malevolent persons' had 'compelled her' to take her religious vows, a situation which 'both in public and in private she had always protested against'. As soon as she was released from these vows, therefore, she considered herself free to marry John Foster, the abbey steward – who in the meantime had been worked on by the same unnamed bullies 'by their threats to become a priest'.

The couple lived a married life 'for sometime' at Baddesley, near Romsey, until objections were made that it was against the law and then her husband 'denied his marital obligations'. The petition did not mention their children, Edward, Andrew and Jane. However, the two years between the suppression of Romsey Abbey and John Foster's cessation of conjugal duty before the commission of June 1541, would surely have not allowed them long enough to produce three offspring, and so they seem to have overcome the early problems in gaining acceptance of their marriage and been left in peace to settle to their family life.

The fate of the other Romsey nuns is not even partly known. Their names, and that of Abbess Elizabeth Ryprose did not appear on a pension list. As shown vividly in the Seventh Episode of a play performed during a pageant to mark Romsey's *Millenary Celebration* in 1907, the abbey ended its long history abruptly by being declared 'dissolved and forfeit to the Crown'. Jane Wadham, John Foster, the Abbess and nuns appeared as characters in the play. The King's commissioner, Dr Layton, rebuffed the Abbess for 'wrongful use' of abbey property and disloyalty to the King because she admitted granting to 'poor folk who, for long service in their latter days have scanty pensions from our revenues'. In reality, one of these had been her own handmaiden, Mrs Short, and husband Christopher, who was also an abbey servant.

Romsey Abbey, Hampshire:
the Abbey Seal and magnificent church

The hard-hearted Layton, as portrayed in the play, told the Abbess to 'get thee hence'. 'Hence!' she wept. 'Whither?' and reminded him that her family and friends were 'but faint echoes of a world renounced'. But the nuns' attempts to go back inside the abbey through its gateway were stopped by soldiers accompanying Layton, and the entrance was boarded up as the nuns then turned sadly away.

Jane Wadham's nephew, Nicholas, was the founder of Wadham College, Oxford. The marriage of her niece – his sister, Margaret – to Nicholas Martin of Athelhampton House in Dorset had wide-ranging effects too, beyond the personal level. This brought all the Wadhams into kinship with one of Dame Elizabeth Shelley's nuns at the Nunnaminster, Mary Martin, and eventually with a former altar-boy called Peter Tichborne, who had served at Masses there. His son, Chideock Tichborne, married Jane Martin, one of Margaret's and Nicholas's four daughters and co-heiresses to Athelhampton. Unfortunately, Jane Martin's husband was a close friend of the Catholic conspirator, Anthony Babington, and he took part in the Babington Plot, which was aimed at assassinating Queen Elizabeth and freeing the captive Mary Queen of Scots to place her on the English throne instead. Chideock was executed with Babington in 1586, in a particularly barbaric way. Early in 1587, the Queen of Scots was also executed, an event of such national and international significance that revenge came in the following year with the mighty Spanish Armada and its failed attempt to invade England.

Through all these great events, one ex-nun is known to have continued living in Bristol on her annual £5 pension. She was 'the faire yong woman of Laycok', Mary Denys, who became Prioress of Kington St Michael nunnery when Cecily Bodenham left there to be the last Abbess of Wilton. Mary survived until 1593, fifty-seven years after the vanished world, in which one of her priory's neighbours, called Old Jacques, had witnessed and praised the teaching work of her nuns.

CHAPTER 3

Dame Bountiful Bonaventure

The well-known saying, 'all at sixes and sevens' has tenuous links with a Cornish lady, whose life was much the opposite of the meaning of this phrase. Thomasine Bonaventure was born in the mid-15th century at the village of Week St Mary, near Bude on the north coast of Cornwall. Through her marriages, she was closely associated with the London Company of Merchant Taylors. She was living in London in the year before the Tudor Age, 1484, when the rivalry between this company and another, representing the Skinners, over their order of precedence in processions was at last resolved. They agreed to alternate the positions of sixth and seventh places between them each year, a custom which has prevailed ever since then.

Thomasine's upbringing in the late medieval Catholic tradition, with its emphasis on good works, clearly influenced all her acts of benevolence as an adult in early Tudor times. She was also motivated by a great love for her native county, so wild and remote then. No other county in the very different 'up country' parts of the kingdom beyond Cornwall could boast so many places named after saints. But Thomasine found that her destiny was to go into that unfamiliar, 'up country' world. A legend about her was published even before the end of the Tudor period, in Richard Carew's *Survey of Cornwall*, and told of a chance encounter which changed her life.

The story stated that she was a young shepherdess tending her flock one day on the moors near Week St Mary, when a London merchant, who was travelling in the West Country, stopped to speak to her as he passed by. He was so impressed with Thomasine that he offered her a place as a servant in his household, and after her 'poore parents' gave their permission, she set off with the merchant for her new life in London. His wife predeceased him, so he then married Thomasine, but before long his own demise left her as a wealthy widow while she was still young.

Carew wrote that Thomasine's second husband was 'one Henry Galle'. However, another part of the Catholic tradition was the importance of Masses for the souls of the dead, and many years later, the detailed arrangements which she included in her will for ceremonies for the repose of her own soul, those of her parents John and Joan, and of her husbands, shows that Henry Galle was her first husband and the name of her second was Thomas Barnaby.

A different picture from the legend also emerges with regard to her family background. John and Joan Bonaventure had two other daughters, Margaret and Alice, besides Thomasine, and two sons, Richard and John. They were not 'poore', for Joan and her sister, Elizabeth Westlake, were co-heiresses to their father's estate. After Elizabeth's marriage into a Devon gentry family, the Dinhams of Woodham Manor, Lifton, these two sisters and their families retained close ties of affection. One of Elizabeth's sons, John, married Joan's granddaughter Margery, a union which was ultimately to aid Thomasine Bonaventure's 'works no less bountiful than charitable'. Thomasine herself remained very much part of her fond, supportive family network long after leaving the West Country for London.

Although many of her relatives continued living in Cornwall and Devon, others also moved to the London area, most notably her clergyman brother, Richard, who was rector of Chelsfield in Kent. Her parents apparently moved to his parish, where they are known to have been buried. A friend of Richard Bonaventure was an affluent London tailor called Richard Nordon, whose business was recorded as supplying customers in Cornwall. Modern studies have put forward the possibility that Thomasine's move to London was more family oriented than portrayed in the legend and, as a result of her brother's introduction, she entered into service in his tailor friend's household. This would also have involved belonging to the well-established local community of tailors, of which her future husbands were members.

Fact and legend about Thomasine are both consistently in accord about her ability and intelligence. Both Henry Galle and Thomas Barnaby were consistent too, in leaving all their property to her when they died – far more than the third usually settled on widows. Historians have interpreted this as an expression of their faith in her to continue their profitable tailoring business. Thomasine would have had the opportunity of learning craft and business skills during her marriages. Her attention to detail in earthly, as well as spiritual matters, was indeed profound and thorough in her own will, so long after her first and second periods of widowhood. Such an aptitude was undoubtedly a great practical asset, and when combined with useful skills, it formed a strong level of competence in running a business. She was, as the 19th-century book on *Cornish Worthies* said of her, a 'Golden Widow'.

Like Thomasine herself, the man named correctly in the legend as her 'third and last' husband was not London-born. John Percival, or Percyvale, came from Cheshire and was 'Maister of the Merchant-taillours' Company when the Tudor Age began. He served London in various official roles too, such as Sheriff, an alderman and Lord Mayor, so Thomasine's expertise in supervising the tailoring business was invaluable during his frequent times on civic duties.

Documents began referring to Thomasine as 'Dame', or sometimes 'Lady Percival' after her husband was knighted by Henry VII in 1487. Sir John Percival's election as Lord Mayor of London, in 1498, had the King's approval, though he probably knew of the Lady Mayoress Thomasine's charitable work in her beloved Cornwall, which had been the scene of serious unrest the previous year. A rebellion against him was defeated, followed by an attempt to dethrone him, which also failed. A Flemish imposter called Perkin Warbeck, who had claimed to be the rightful King, was captured.

Warbeck's wife was a beautiful Scottish noblewoman, Lady Catherine Gordon, a kinswoman of Henry VII, his mother and also King James IV of Scotland. She was left in the Cornish castle at St Michael's Mount during her husband's 'invasion', but taken prisoner there by the Tudor King's soldiers and despite her rank, she was brought before him at Exeter, tied up as if she belonged to the lowest rank, a bondswoman. King Henry soon freed her and gave her an honourable escort of ladies to take her to join Queen Elizabeth of York's household, where she was treated with due respect and dignity. Warbeck was later executed, but Lady Catherine remained happily in England for the rest of her life – another forty years, during which she remarried three times!

Carew's *Survey of Cornwall* summed up the diverse range of Thomasine's generosity: 'repairing of highways, building of bridges, endowing of maidens, relieving of prisoners, feeding and apparelling the poor etc. Among the rest, at this St Mary Wike [Week St Mary] she founded a chantry and free-school, together with fair lodgings for the schoolmasters, scholars and officers …' She was said to have 'caused to be erected … a substantial bridge' at Week Ford in her native parish, to honour the memory of her first husband, and 'to have constructed a good new road down to the coast' to mark her third husband's election as Lord Mayor of London. Yet her donations of money to nunneries reflected her attachment to London, as well as the West Country. The London priories of Clerkenwell, Holywell and St Helen's in Bishopgate benefited from her support, along with Cornworthy Priory in South Devon.

Thomasine and John Percival were also very loyal to their craft and guild. Both gave property to the Merchant Taylors Company, to fund a charity which was set up partly to help the poor of their parish of St Mary Wolnoth, London. They each founded a grammar school too, in their respective places of birth. Thomasine had no children by any of her marriages, but before Henry VIII's reign began in 1509, her grammar school near the village church at Week St Mary was the only one established by a woman who was not of exalted noble rank. Its establishment took place during 'her last widdowhood' and was indeed a tribute to her happy, ongoing relationship with kinsfolk still living in the West Country, in particular her Devonshire cousin, John Dinham, and his wife, her Cornish niece Margery. They had succeeded to his family's Woodham Manor ancestral home in Lifton, where they dwelt about twelve miles from Thomasine's school.

Her will revealed that cousin John, also her nephew by marriage, was very much her man-on-the-spot, providing the necessary local supervision of matters with regard to the school. Thomasine had certainly been able to offer him a powerful incentive to do so on her behalf – the prospect of bequeathing to him all the residue of her accumulated wealth. And that was exactly what she did, in warm-hearted words expressing her complete assurance in him to implement the practical set-up of 'my gramer schoole' according to her wishes. Margery Dinham received several 'best' items from Thomasine and the children of this inter-generational couple were provided with financial gifts.

Amongst other family members who received bequests from Thomasine was her brother, John Bonaventure, who became a Mayor himself, of Launceston in Cornwall. Her goddaughter, Thomasine Baker, who was probably named after her, was awarded an extra sum of money above the amount bequeathed to her. So too was a favourite servant called Margaret Lawson. Dame Thomasine's other bequests were numerous to servants, apprentices past and present, and children from poor families who were receiving education in her large London household. Characteristically, she made thoughtful, conscientious arrangements for her executors to continue to look after these children's board, lodging and learning after her death. Such a level of consideration extended also to other household members, the very people who shared her day-to-day existence. Some later accounts of her life stated that she retired to Cornwall for her final years, but her will, so outstanding for its depth of detail, made no mention of this.

Thomasine died in 1512, having survived her third husband, Sir John, for nine years. She was buried beside him in the chapel of the Merchant Taylors' patron saint, John the Baptist, at St Mary Wolnoth Church. Some of the buildings of her school and chantry still stand as cottages at Week St Mary. Above a doorway is a personal remembrance of her, in the form of a large letter **T** – believed to be for Thomasine – on a piece of carved granite stonework. Carew wrote of her school that 'as the bent of her desire was holy, so God blessed the same with all wished success'. It earned due praise in a report of 1545 as 'a great comfort to all the county'.

Carving of the initial 'T' for Thomasine above the doorway at her school in Week St Mary

At the end of that year, a new law targeted chantries for suppression and so the endowments left by Thomasine to provide payment for priests at her chantry to pray for her soul, and those of her husbands and parents, were transferred to the King's coffers. The school went into a rapid decline 'owing ... to its being in a desolate place' and it too was transferred, to the larger parish of Launceston.

The West Country was literally 'up in arms' as a result of bitter opposition there to more religious reforms. Disturbances in 1547 and 1548 preceded another serious, but failed rebellion, during the following year. The restoration of chantries and prayers for the dead were amongst the rebels' demands, along with the 'olde services ... in Latten, not English'. Cornishmen complained that some of them did not understand English. Its compulsory use in 'newe' religious services heightened fears for the loss of their own Cornish language.

Although the grammar school at Week St Mary lasted for less than half a century, their remarkable great lady, Thomasine Bonaventure - whose name was superbly suited to her 'bountiful workes' - has an enduring place in history through the story of the Cornish Shepherdess.

CHAPTER 4

'Of Myne Owne Authority'

The ancient Forest of Wychwood in Oxfordshire was long reputed to be one of the most notorious haunts of ghosts, witches and enchantments in England. A strange and spooky atmosphere still lingers in its dark woodlands, which probably provided some inspiration for the Oxford author, J.R.R. Tolkien, who used the name of the local river Evenlode in his classic tale, *The Lord of the Rings*. The surviving part of Wychwood Forest is small, but not surprisingly it is linked with a ghost story about a Tudor lady whose tragic death has never been fully solved.

A tradition of the area told that the spirit of Amy Robsart, the first wife of Queen Elizabeth's favourite, Robert Dudley, frequented the main avenue of approach called the Broad Light, towards his house at Cornbury Park, which is adjacent to the Forest – and for people who were unlucky to see her, that was a sign of their own impending death. Robert Dudley himself was ailing when he rode through the Broad Light at dusk one evening in late August 1588 and the portent of doom, Amy's ghost, appeared to him and informed him that he would join her in ten days' time.

A few weeks earlier, he had been actively involved in the victory over the Spanish Armada, but amid the celebrations the Queen had sent him to take the waters at Buxton for the sake of his health and he was on his way there when he stayed to rest at Cornbury Park. His previous stopping-place had been at Rycote, near Thame, the home of Elizabeth's close friend, Lady Norris, and from there he wrote to the Queen and thanked her for some medicine she had given him, which had helped him to feel better. She placed his message amongst her most treasured personal possessions, with her own words added – 'His last letter' – for his illness worsened at Cornbury and he died there on 4th September.

Four days later was the 28th anniversary of Amy Robsart's death in 1560.

Amy's ghost seems to have been an unquiet spirit, not only restless but mobile too. Soon after she died at Cumnor Place, near Oxford, she was said to haunt her childhood home over 100 miles away at Syderstone Hall, Norfolk, close to the ancient shrine at Walsingham. And when this house was demolished, off she went to cause some ghostly goings-on at nearby Syderstone rectory. Yet there was a tradition at Cumnor that 'Madame Dudley's ghost' also 'did use to walk in Cumnor Park and that it walked so obstinately' that 'no less than nine parsons from Oxford' were required to exorcise her. They 'at last laid her in a pond called Madam Dudley's Pond and … the water in that pond was never known to freeze afterwards'.

The village church at Syderstone has another reminder of Amy, with her initials, A R on the churchyard gate, and inside Cumnor Church, letters written by her are displayed near a large statue of Queen Elizabeth. These letters were published in the *Wiltshire Archaeological Journal* as long ago as 1878. The wording of one of them shows a young woman who was in love with her husband: 'although I forgot to move my lord thereof before his departing, he being sore troubled with weighty affairs, and I not being all together in quiet for his sudden departing …'

Amy was corresponding with a steward called Mr Flowerdew at Syderstone, where there was a large sheep-farm which she had inherited from her father, Sir John Robsart. Because of the laws which regarded married women's property as belonging to their husbands, however, Flowerdew had sent two letters to Robert Dudley about matters relating to the farm and some poor people who were waiting for their payment. Amy replied with a courteous apology for Robert's lack of response, due to being called away on his 'weighty' business. She then gave the go-ahead to Flowerdew to sell some wool, even at a loss, so that the poor would not be kept waiting any longer for their money:

Cumnor Church, Oxfordshire

'I neither may nor can deny you that request in my lord's absence, of myne owne authority ... desiring you further that you will make sale of the wool as soon as is possible ... for my lord so earnestly required me at his departing to see those poor men satisfied, as though it had been a matter depending on life, wherefore I force not to sustain a little loss ...'

This letter was dated 7th August, but no year was given, though it is thought to be 1559, during the first year of Elizabeth's reign, when Robert's duties as her Master of Horse would have required almost continual attendance at Court. Amy ended her letter 'from Mr Hyde's house', which was at Denchworth, in the Vale of the White Horse in Oxfordshire. Her husband's account books reveal that she lived with her friends there for long periods and he made frequent visits to see her.

Amy's other letter also had an August date, the 24th, and may have been written in 1560, two weeks before she died. It was penned 'at Cumnore' to her London tailor, William Edney:

> *'With my heartiest commendations, these shall be to desire*
> *you to take pains for me as to make this gown of velvet, which*
> *I send you, such a collar as you made my russet taffeta gown*
> *you sent me last ... I pray you let it be done with as much*
> *speed as you can and sent by this bearer, Frewin, the carrier*
> *of Oxford, and thus I bid you most heartily farewell ...'*

An inventory of her wardrobe tells of her liking for warm colours, such as russet, crimson and scarlet for gowns, petticoats, 'round kirtles', and ribbon and fringe trimmings. Amy was also fond of visiting friends in Lincolnshire, Suffolk, Hampshire and London. Having no children of her own, or the responsibilities of running a great household, perhaps she preferred a mainly country life, enjoying the company of her friends, to a more formal, potentially lonely life at Court.

Mr Hyde's widowed sister, Mrs Odingsells, went with Amy as her companion when she took up residence at Cumnor Place towards the end of 1559. Her apartments in this medieval manor house were situated near those of a lady from the owner's family, Mrs Owens, and a different wing of the house was rented by Robert Dudley's steward, Anthony Forster, and his wife Anne.

Although neither of Amy's letters hint at any illness of hers, the Spanish ambassador, Count de Feria, reported in the early weeks of Elizabeth's reign that Lord Robert's wife was suffering from a malady in one of her breasts – usually assumed to be breast cancer. Her health was probably further undermined by the distressing gossip and rumours which swiftly began to circulate about the new Queen's romance with Robert Dudley. Amy must surely have heard so many of these which posed an ominous threat to her. A frequent rumour, for instance, was that she was thought to be the only hindrance to marriage between her husband and Elizabeth, so she would have to be removed, either by divorce or poison, which Robert had already arranged. An alternative tale also went around that the Queen was waiting for Amy to die soon of a terminal illness.

On 8th September 1560, a Sunday, a Fair was being held in the nearby town of Abingdon. Amy decided to dine with Mrs Owens that day and ordered all her servants to visit the Fair, which was generally 'thought a very strange thing for her to do'. Mrs Odingsells spoke out against this order, and Amy replied angrily that she could please herself 'but all *her* people should go'. And away they went, only to return to Cumnor that evening and find Amy's body on the floor of the hall, at the foot of a staircase. Her neck had been broken.

Robert Dudley was then with the Court at Windsor Castle, forty miles from Cumnor. A messenger came to him

Amy's fatal fall

the next day, 'by whom I do understand that my wife is dead, and as he saithe, by a fall from a pair of staires'. He went on in his letter to one of his officials, Sir Thomas Blount, 'The greatness and suddennesse of the misfortune doth so perplex me ... I have no waie to purge myself of the malicious talke that I knowe the wicked worlde will use ...' He sent Blount to Cumnor to investigate the circumstances surrounding Amy's death, and also to set up a coroner's inquest immediately. Then he added, 'send me your trewe opinion of that matter, whether it happened by evill chance, or villainye ...'

Blount asked an innkeeper in Abingdon what local opinions were being expressed about Amy's death. "Some said well, and some said evil," was the reply, and his own personal view was that it was misfortune, because Anthony Forster was well-respected in the area and "no-one would believe a crime could be committed in his house".

Amy's maid, Mrs Pinto, answered Blount's enquiries with greater first-hand knowledge, "By my faith, I judge it chance, and neither done by man nor by herself: for she was a good virtuous gentlewoman, and daily would pray upon her knees, and divers times I have heard her pray to God to deliver her from desperation." When Blount suggested that perhaps Amy had thought of suicide, the maid said, "No, good Mr Blount, do not so judge of my words. If you do so gather, I am sorry I said so much."

Sir Thomas Blount acknowledged to Amy's husband that Mrs Pinto was devoted to her. This maid who knew her so well, and was in her company so much that she often overheard Amy's private prayers, probably took great care of her mistress. Even so, Mrs Pinto was still sent to Abingdon Fair with all the other servants on that Sunday. In the very situation of being at close quarters with other people for most of the time, though, may be a possible clue to the mystery of Amy's 'strange' behaviour then: perhaps in her 'desperation', she simply wished for some quiet, personal time of peace and solitude, away from the inevitable noise of her household for a while, and especially away from the rumours about her and Robert and the Queen.

Privacy was a luxury in Tudor times, however, but the hope of finding some may even have been almost second nature to Amy. Her crucial, formative years had been spent in the pre-Reformation Catholic world at a time when thousands of pilgrims still flocked past her home village each year to nearby Walsingham. Many of them would have been on their own individual quest for the Virgin Mary's help, a quest which could give brief, reflective periods of solitude, free from social contact, in the county of Norfolk with its long-established reputation for female recluses.

The inquest on Amy returned a verdict of accidental death. But Sir Thomas Blount's impression that she had been beset by a very poor state of mind, grew with further fact-finding in and around Cumnor. Advances in medical knowledge led to some modern studies of Amy's story agreeing with the result of the inquest and also trying to explain the mystery of her fall. The spread of breast cancer to other parts of her body would have impaired her sense of balance and caused her bones, especially her spine, to become more brittle – a lethal combination if she was ever to lose her footing.

Recent studies, however, have tended to dismiss this weakened, fragile frame idea and re-asserted that Amy was murdered, a view based on the discovery of the original inquest report. This document revealed that she suffered serious head injuries, apparently consistent with being struck by a weapon, rather than the impact of the hard, and probably sharp-edged, stone stairs which she descended so tragically.

According to the usual practice for husbands of great ladies in Tudor times, Robert Dudley did not attend the magnificent funeral for Amy at St Mary's Church, Oxford, but 'many mornars in blake' were there and also four royal heralds, who displayed 'a grett baner of armes'. Shortly afterwards, a letter of condolence was sent to Robert by the English ambassador to France, Sir Nicholas Throckmorton:

'I understand of the cruel mischance late happened to my lady your late bedfellow ...' He hoped that his letter would not renew Robert's grief.

By the end of October, however, the 'malicious talke' so dreaded by Robert Dudley was rife. In England, some of Elizabeth's beloved people said openly that they wanted no more women rulers, and in France, her ambassador, Throckmorton, complained of 'being weary' of his life because 'so evil be the reports as I am ashamed to write them'. Amy's death, so widely expected in rumours beforehand, was regarded as too much of a coincidence to prevent a vehement backlash afterwards, whatever the official verdict of the inquest. Suspicions continued to cloud her husband's life and resurfaced occasionally as slanders such as that spread by her own half-brother, John Appleyard, seven years later. He waited until then before claiming dissatisfaction with the verdict and 'that for the sake of Dudley, he had covered the murder of his sister'. He later admitted that he had lied and 'cravyd of pardon'. Appleyard's slander had probably been a means of revenge for Robert's lack of help towards him concerning a Norfolk manor.

The murder stories persisted in different versions, including one tale of Anthony Forster sending Amy's servants out of the house, before murdering Amy, on Robert's orders, by throwing her down the stairs. Forster, who had not even been at Cumnor on the day she died, appeared as joint murderer in another version with a knight called Sir Richard Verney, who was not even mentioned in contemporary documents. He was the arch-villain, though, in Sir Walter Scott's novel, *Kenilworth,* in which Amy was strangled before her body fell through a trapdoor. Scott acknowledged that the basis of his story came from the 17th-century author, Elias Ashmole, whose book on the *Antiquities of Berkshire* was itself influenced by a slanderous publication of 1584, called *Leicester's Commonwealth,* which dredged up various scandals about Robert. Its title referred to his earldom of Leicester, which Elizabeth had conferred upon him twenty years earlier.

A similar tale lingered in the area around a North Yorkshire manor, once owned by Robert. Hackness, near Scarborough, was purchased for a young heiress named Margaret Dakyns about a year after Robert Dudley's reputed encounter with the ghost of Amy at Cornbury Park. Margaret's first husband was Robert's stepson, Walter Devereux, and her second was his nephew, Thomas Sidney, both of whom died before she was twenty-five.

The novel *Eventide Light* by Emma Marshall, published in 1890, included a scene in which Margaret's third husband, Sir Thomas Posthumous Hoby, gave his ailing wife an angry push down a flight of stairs, to hasten her to greet the arrival of visitors. She fell so heavily that when she landed at the foot of the stairs, her forehead was bleeding from a cut which did not have chance to heal, as she was too frail to recover from the shock of her fall and soon 'passed away like a tired child ready for slumber'. When her famous *Diary of Lady Margaret Hoby* was published in 1930, its editor, D.M. Meads, referred to the ongoing legend that Hoby speeded Margaret's death by kicking her downstairs and that her bloodstains caused by her fall could not be removed. She did predecease Hoby, but the epitaph he wrote for her memorial in the village church at Hackness is one of praise for her 'godly manner of life and conversation'. Like Robert Dudley, Hoby was an unpopular man, and a ready target for a tale of wife-killing to add to his low reputation.

On a happier note for future generations, both Lady Amy Dudley, with her letters, and Lady Margaret Hoby, with her diary, left behind them glimpses of the Tudor world as seen through their own eyes.

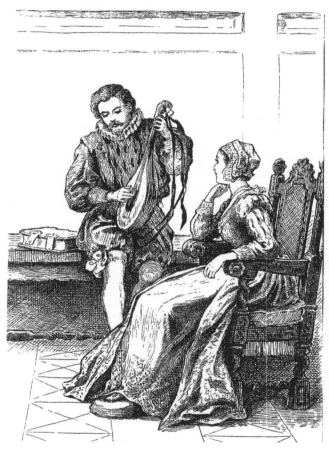

A scene from Eventide Light: *Lady Margaret Hoby with her second husband, Thomas Sidney*

CHAPTER 5

Mam Cymru – Mother of Wales

Celtic connections were rooted deeply in the family tree of a lady of romance in Welsh history. Katherine of Berain, who was born around 1535, inherited from her half-Breton, half-Welsh mother, Jane Veleville, the Tudors' medieval ancestral home of Plas Penmynydd on the Isle of Anglesey. Her Breton grandfather, Sir Roland de Veleville, had been rewarded by Henry VII with property in north-west Wales, including Penmynydd. Such a sign of the King's high esteem has long been reputed to point also to Sir Roland being of royal Tudor blood, as Henry's illegitimate son born during the King's youthful years of exile in Brittany.

Katherine of Berain

Katherine's maiden surname was indeed Tudor, but not from any royal ancestry. It came instead from her Welsh father, Tudur ap Robert Vychan of Berain, near Denbigh, in north-east Wales, from whom she also inherited considerable lands. Welsh bards wrote and recited their praises of her in her native language, and she became known as 'Mam Cymru', the 'Mother of Wales', because so many of the country's families are descended from her. She acquired in turn the surnames Salusbury, Clough, Wynn and Thelwall from her marriages into three distinguished Denbighshire families and one from the Conwy valley in north-west Wales.

One of Katherine's descendants was an 18th-century travel writer called Thomas Pennant, who recounted a whimsical tale from popular tradition about her and the first three spouses. At the funeral of her first husband, John Salusbury, in Llannefydd Church, near Berain, in 1566, Katherine was led into the service with her arm linked through that of Sir Richard Clough, a local financier. She was later escorted out of the church in a similar way by Maurice Gwynn of Gwydir Castle, Conwy, who took the opportunity to propose to her. Katherine declined his offer very politely, informing him that she had already accepted Sir Richard's proposal as they went into the church! But she reassured Maurice Wynn that if she was widowed for a second time, she would remember him. Only six or seven years later, she was 'as good as her word', and when she married Wynn, she became the third wife of her third husband. Pennant wrote that he was descended from this marriage.

Other North Wales tales about Katherine of Berain include oft-quoted accounts of her molten lead trick. Her popularity was said to have been such that she attracted several lovers in addition to her husbands and whenever she tired of them, she killed them by pouring this substance into their ears while they slept. She was even alleged to have buried some of them in her orchard at Berain. Tradition also explained that her fourth husband, Edward Thelwall, outlived Katherine because he realized her love for him was fading, so he avoided his predecessors' fate by shutting her away in a room at Berain and starving her to death.

Katherine married the Denbighshire heir, John Salusbury, in 1557. His father was known as 'Sir John of the Thumbs' because he had two thumbs on each hand! The Salusburys, whose ancestral home was at Llewenny, near Denbigh, were a prominent local family. Early in Queen Elizabeth's reign, however, two of them were executed for pulling down hedges and fences which enclosed land owned by the Lord of Denbigh, a man who was another reputed spouse-murderer and much hated in the county – the royal favourite, Robert Dudley.

The Salusbury marriage produced two sons, Thomas and John, who were both infants when their father died. They may have been entrusted to their grandparents' care at Llewenny during Katherine's second marriage. Her new husband, Sir Richard Clough, had business interests overseas and she dwelt with him in Antwerp and Hamburg. They had two daughters, Anne and Mary, but Katherine was again widowed in 1570. The pattern of two offspring by each husband continued after she married Maurice Wynn, her family then being completed with their son, Edward, and daughter, Jane.

Maurice Wynn was depicted by his eldest son, John, as an easily dominated man. An impassioned letter from Katherine to John Wynn revealed all too clearly who was capable of dominating his father! She described herself as 'a woman foolish and fond', but some of her words indicated a more managing disposition at work. She was seeking stepson John's help with Robert Dudley on behalf of one of her kinsmen, a former servant, 'specially to make my lord conceive the matter aright … wherein you shall do unto me a most acceptable pleasure and to your father and yourself much credit …'

Her use of flattery with her stepson to 'make' Robert Dudley see the situation according to her 'aright' point of view found no courteous opinion of her in John Wynn. With some resentment, he later referred to Katherine of Berain and her first mother-in-law, Lady Jane Salusbury, as 'the sirens which enchant' his father because 'they so rule my father, that he ratifieth what they think fit to be done'.

Lady Salusbury ensured that this episode of ruling and ratifying took place in her home surroundings at Llewenny. A marriage was arranged between two children – Katherine's eldest son, Thomas Salusbury, the heir to both Berain and Llewenny, and Maurice Wynn's daughter, Margaret. The local churches formed part of the diocese of the Bishops of Chester, where child marriages and even divorces were fairly customary in Elizabethan times. Katherine had spoken of her 'poor child', 'little Thomas Salusbury', in her letter to John Wynn as being prone to 'great perplexity' and distress. He undoubtedly suffered these over his match with Margaret Wynn, from which he 'utterly dissented'.

But those 'sirens', his mother and grandmother, were a formidable combined force. They were probably trying to outwit Robert Dudley from becoming Thomas's legal guardian when his grandfather, 'Sir John of the Thumbs', died. Their wishes prevailed, despite his feelings of aversion and the doubts of some of their menfolk about the match. A celebration to mark their agreement to the marriage contract was held at Gwydir Castle, and Katherine's reluctant son was duly forced into his hated wedlock in about 1578.

Reaction eventually set in against such petticoat law, when Thomas was sent to study at Oxford. He formed friendships with other students, including one called Anthony Babington, whose influence unfortunately caused him to take part in the disastrous Babington Plot (mentioned in Chapter 2). Thomas was executed for treason in 1586, leaving a nine-month old daughter, Margaret, who later married into the Norris family of Speke Hall, near Liverpool.

Amid the family grief after the eldest son's death as a traitor, relations between the 'sirens' became much cooler. Perhaps they partly blamed each other for the tragedy. Property matters also needed to be resolved over what should have been Thomas Salusbury's inheritance. Royal officials investigated whether any of this could be forfeited to the Crown in the usual way in cases of treason, but as he had not yet succeeded to any of his mother's or grandparents' properties, these remained within the family. Katherine settled her Berain property on Thomas's daughter and her Anglesey estates and Llewenny became the inheritance of her second son, John Salusbury.

She was, by this time, married to her fourth husband, Edward Thelwall. But her new heir's marriage was of more immediate concern, for if John had a legitimate male heir of his own, this would secure the properties and especially prevent any risk of one of his Salusbury uncles from succeeding to Llewenny. Katherine therefore fast-tracked his marriage only three months after her eldest son's death. A great Christmas festive gathering was held at Berain in 1586, to celebrate the wedding of John Salusbury and Ursula Stanley, an illegitimate daughter of the Earl of Derby and his long-established mistress, Joan Halsall. Ursula was born around the time that her father's unhappy marriage to Katherine's royal cousin, Lady Margaret Clifford (mentioned in Chapter 1), finally broke down. The bride's own nuptial ceremony, however, was followed by the performance of a masque, in which poets were busy eulogizing her new mother-in-law:

> *'Dame Venus deare you may rejoice*
> *At your sonne Cupides happy choyse ...'*

Katherine of Berain was very fortunate that her hasty matching of her second son contrasted so greatly with that of his older brother, Thomas. John Salusbury's happy marriage to Ursula lived up to its description in the poem. A more contented character than his brother, John worked hard to rehabilitate his family from the shadow of treason, which had been begun by the scheming of his mother and grandmother. He was a poet himself, and one of several Welsh country gentlemen who actively encouraged the Welsh language, literature and love of prehistoric sites. He and Ursula had their surviving son and heir in 1589. Twelve years later, a book of poetry was published in honour of their successful marriage and included poems contributed by Shakespeare and Ben Jonson.

The marriage arrangements for Katherine's other offspring pointed to a possible lesson learnt after the sorrow over Thomas's death, for her youngest son, Edward Wynn, followed John's example and married into a family not connected with any of his stepfathers. Edward's wife was Blanche Vaughan, who came from a leading South Wales family. Katherine's three daughters, however, were all allied to close kin from her first, third and fourth marriages: Anne Clough married into the Salusbury family, Mary Clough into the Wynns and ten year old Jane Wynn was wedded to Edward Thelwall's twelve year old son and heir, Simon.

An elegy about Katherine noted that she was at the Thelwalls' home, Plas-y-Ward, near Ruthin, when she died in August 1591 – not at Berain itself, as stated in local tradition. She was buried at Llannefydd Church, without a monument raised by her progeny to commemorate her. This neglect has been viewed as so remiss that it has caused considerable comment in subsequent centuries.

Her bards, including one called Sion Tudor, paid much tribute, though, in their elegies to this great lady who had been their patroness. Another of them, Rhysiart Phylip, wrote one in Welsh of her kindness to poor and hungry people who sought help 'at her door'. As he concluded with regard to Katherine of Berain, 'it is right that she should be remembered'.

CHAPTER 6

Nuns of Vales and Dales

Yorkshire had so many more nunneries than any other English county, that perhaps not surprisingly, it was unique also for its higher proportion of naughty nuns. Choirstalls surviving from long before Tudor times at the priory of Swine-in-Holderness, in East Yorkshire, even have a carving of a nun's face partly veiled, with one eye covered, yet described as seeming to wink with the other eye!

Medieval carving of a nun's face, Swine Priory

Saintly apparel such as a tunic and several girdles were amongst a motley assortment of sacred relics, which Yorkshire abbeys and priories offered as aids to comfort women facing the ordeal of childbirth. Not that any of these items were intended to be used by nuns, of course, least of all by a prioress. Early in Henry VII's reign, though, Prioress Elizabeth Popeley of Arthington Priory, near Leeds, had the chance of testing a precious relic called Our Lady's girdle when she gave birth at the nunnery.

Medieval paintings and stained glass windows sometimes depict this relic, which five of the 'White Rose' county's religious houses claimed to possess. Arthington was the only nunnery amongst these and ironically, it belonged to the very strict Cluniac religious order. The errant Elizabeth Popeley was deprived of office, and not only lost the privilege of her private Prioress's chamber but also was barred from voting in the election for her successor.

Only a few other Yorkshire nunneries could boast a separate chamber for their prioress, though sometimes with unglazed windows, for they were small and mostly poverty-stricken establishments. Often, however, they were only a few miles distant from each other, which was a real boon over the centuries, especially for female travellers such as pilgrims in need of their hospitality and shelter. These sanctuaries could be found along routes which converged from hills, dales, moors, wolds, coastal areas and the lowland Vale of Pickering into the broad acres of the Vale of York and the historic city of York itself, at the very centre of the county which bears its name. About 260 Yorkshire nuns were turned out of their convents at the Dissolution of the Monasteries - over a sixth of the national total.

The nuns of vales and dales mainly belonged to the Cistercian and Benedictine religious orders, and there was also a community of Gilbertine nuns and canons at Watton Priory in East Yorkshire. They were evidently very sociable ladies, whichever order ruled them. Downstream from the sheltered Lower Wharfedale setting of Arthington, for instance, Prioress Maud Tailbois of Nun Appleton Priory received several 'get thee back to the nunnery' injunctions about her nuns after a visit from the Archbishop of York around the time of Elizabeth Popeley's misdemeanour. 'Item, that none of your sisters use ye ale house,' these declared, 'nor ye waterside, where concourse of strangers daily resort'. The river Wharfe flows into the river Ouse nearby and this major water route to York was a tempting attraction for the nuns, but any unauthorized outings along this were deemed to be strictly off limits: 'item, that the Prioress licence none of your sisters to go on pilgrimage or visit their friends without a great cause ... and then such a sister ... to have with her one of the most sadd and well disposed sisters ...' And if the nuns hoped to counteract these curbs by receiving visitors at the priory instead, especially men, there were further no-go areas: 'item, that none of your sisters bring in, receive or take any laie man, religiose or secular into their chamber or any secrete place, day or night, nor with them in such private places to commune etc. or drinke, without licence of your prioress'.

Anne Langton was in charge at Nun Appleton in 1518, when she also became the guardian of an orphaned local heiress called Isabel Thwaites. Prioress Anne tried to impose the same restrictions on young Isabel as those designed for her nuns. She especially forbade visits to the nunnery by a youth called William Fairfax. But the old saying that 'neither walls nor waters can separate lovers' came true for Isabel and William – at least with regard to walls, for he broke into Nun Appleton one night by climbing the outer wall. Isabel then fled with him to Bolton Percy Church, about two miles away, where they married at once, before the Prioress could stop them.

At the time of their escapade, the Prioress of Esholt Priory, in neighbouring Airedale, was Elizabeth Pudsey. Her nuns did more than 'use ye ale house' – these enterprising ladies brewed their own ale next to their kitchen and sold any that was surplus to their requirements. Perhaps inevitably, a visit to Esholt by the Archbishop's vicar-general, Dr Clyff, in the mid-1530s resulted in the instruction 'that the prioresse suffer no alehouse to be kept within the precinct of the gates of the saide monasterie'. The nuns' brewhouse was apparently still working, though, on the summer day when the priory was closed in 1539.

Other bones of contention mentioned by Dr Clyff led to injunctions similar to those many years before at Nun Appleton regarding male visitors. And a lack of sufficient security at Esholt meant that a high wall was to be built 'without delay' to close access into the priory from a public way which went towards the river Aire and a 'fair bridge', which the prioress, as 'the lady' of this part of the river 'must maintain' in good repair. The new wall was to be a barrier to 'many ills that may be committed'.

On that theme, however, one of the young Esholt nuns, Dame Joan Hutton, had already committed a 'horrible crime' and was given a two-year punishment for her 'ill example to other religious persons' of having a 'child of her body begotten'. She was to be imprisoned or kept in a secret chamber within the nuns' dormitory, no-one was allowed to speak to her without the prioress's permission and she was to undergo penance every Wednesday and Friday with a diet of bread and ale only. Additionally, there was the ominous-sounding prospect of being disciplined in the presence of the other nuns in the chapter-house each Friday for her offence.

Two other nuns were also alleged to have broken their vows of chastity: Agnes Wood, who was still in her twenties, and Agnes Bayne, who was said to have had a child, though she was about fifty and only slightly younger than Dame Joan Hollynraker, who was described in Latin as 'decrepita'. Elizabeth Pudsey, who served as Prioress until 1536, became afflicted in the same way. She was lame, unable to ride and probably too frail to exercise her right to fish 'at her pleasure' in her part of the Aire.

Prioress Elizabeth's family name may provide a possible link with a Tudor tale concerning the North Yorkshire nunnery of Marrick Priory in Swaledale, for an inscription on a floor slab in the church there has been said to mark the grave of a nun called Isabella, 'sister of Thomas Pudsey de Barfort'. The identity of this nun has even been reputed to be that of a royal maid of honour called Isabella Beaufort, who was about nineteen years old when she fled from Court and the amorous advances of Henry VIII and sought sanctuary at Marrick, disguised as a page boy. She was one of many ladies who were the target of the King's attentions during his first two marriages, their very names either unknown to history or long forgotten. Fortunately for Isabella, her situation on arrival at Marrick reflected the name of one of its twelve nuns then, Dame Anne *Ladyman*, rather than one of the others, Dame Margaret *Lovechild*! The Prioress, Christabel Cowper, came from a local family who had lived for generations in the nearby town of Richmond, of which Henry VII and his father, Edmund Tudor, had been the Earl, and his mother, Margaret Beaufort, was its Countess for over half a century. Prioress Christabel soon learnt the details of Isabella's sudden flight from Court in male attire and gave permission for the girl to take refuge at the priory.

A different version of her subsequent life tells of a more romantic fate than becoming one of the sisters at Marrick. Shortly before this nunnery was dissolved in 1539, a distinguished visitor was Joan Darrell, Prioress of Amesbury in Wiltshire, and she chanced to recognize Isabella as the past sweetheart of her own nephew, Edward Herbert of Somerset. Through her efforts, he and Isabella Beaufort were re-united.

Another Prioress Joan was controversially connected with two of the nunneries in the North Yorkshire Moors. The nuns of Rosedale Priory had once been discouraged from an attempt to create a more homely environment amid their wild moorland surroundings, when an Archbishop of York forbade them to allow puppies into their church and choir, because these were distracting them from their services and prayers. Rosedale was situated on one of the shortest routes between York and the port and abbey at Whitby, and so the nuns would have often provided the customary food and shelter for travellers. The priory's fragmentary remains in its very steep-sided valley include a door lintel with a Latin inscription which translates as 'All is vanity', and there are medieval wayside crosses nearby, with names such as Fat Betty, Old Ralph and Young Ralph.

Local legend links these crosses as meeting-places where the prioresses of Rosedale and neighbouring Basedale Priory resolved their disagreements over the boundaries of their lands. In August 1524, a thirty year old nun called Joan Fletcher left Rosedale and journeyed past the crosses to become the new Prioress of Basedale. She took an oath of obedience to Cardinal Wolsey, who was then the absent Archbishop of York. Prioress Joan had her own chamber 'over the west part of the cloyster' at Basedale and this had 'a fayre round bay window glasid' and an inner chamber. Three adjacent chambers were 'called geste chambres'. She appears to have enjoyed the facilities rather too well, possibly succumbing to the temptation to entertain an unnamed male guest in these close quarters – in 1527, she resigned her office, before she could be deprived of it for sinful conduct.

Later documents about her did not give the exact nature of her offence, but hinted strongly that it was a moral lapse. Perhaps she was another mother-nun, and if so, she would have had the chance to avail herself of the relic of the Virgin Mary's milk which Basedale owned 'for lying-in women'. What is known is that she stopped wearing her nun's apparel, then left Basedale and 'lived in the world'. She was replaced as Prioress by Elizabeth Rowghton, formerly a nun at Keldholme Priory, near Kirkbymoorside, a few miles from Rosedale.

Joan Fletcher must have stayed out of her convent for at least three years, though where she lived, and on what money for her upkeep, are details not recorded. Her return to a religious life was some time after the downfall and death of Wolsey in 1530. His successor, Archbishop Lee, sent Joan to her previous priory, Rosedale, to do her penance. All too soon, though, she proved to be a disruptive influence, whose pretence of penitence was, as he put it, a 'sham'. He wrote to Prioress Mary Marshall of Rosedale to send Joan safely at Rosedale's cost back to Basedale, where she could weep over her faults in the place she had committed them. Prioress Elizabeth Rowghton received a letter from Lee at the same time, instructing the nuns to treat 'your late prioress' kindly and pay for her maintenance, but prevent her from leaving Basedale without the new Prioress's permission. However much of a come-down this was for Joan Fletcher in the nunnery she had once headed, she was listed as one of the Basedale nuns when it was dissolved in 1539. Her annual pension was £1, less than a sixth of that awarded to Elizabeth Rowghton.

During the years of Joan Fletcher's misdemeanours, the saga of a young Yorkshire nun highlighted two possible causes of broken vows. Elizabeth Lutton of Little Mareis or Yedingham Priory in the Vale of Pickering reached the age of twenty-seven before she transgressed from her vows, but she had already spent almost half of her short life in the convent. She had taken the veil as a novice at fourteen and then her final vows as a nun at fifteen and she often complained that this had happened against her will.

The various recipients of her tale of woe included an elderly and wealthy local landowner, Sir Robert Constable, when he called in at the priory for a courtesy drink of ale during one of his journeys in 1525. He also went to pray with the nuns in their small church, where he noticed that Elizabeth Lutton was in disgrace and therefore separated from the others. When he sought to know the reason for this, she told him she was pregnant. The priory had three houses within its group of buildings, one of which was 'a little dwellynge house' next to a storehouse. Elizabeth Lutton was literally confined to one of these as punishment until she had her baby. While she waited, there was a change of prioress at Yedingham, from Dame Elizabeth Whitehead to Dame Agnes Bradrigge, who appears to have been professed as a nun at the same time as Elizabeth Lutton. The nuns' confessor prevailed upon her to accept this sinful sister into the community of nuns again after the child was born.

Years of religious life passed by, until suddenly in 1532, Constable re-emerged in Elizabeth's story. A group of his men accompanied a man called Thomas Scaseby on a visit to the nunnery one day – certainly not for courtesy drinks of ale, but to abduct Elizabeth Lutton! They accomplished this with some alacrity, at least on her part, for she so much welcomed the chance of escape. She soon forsook her nuns' vows and made marriage vows with her abductor, Scaseby, who perhaps had fathered her child. Constable's motive in helping the former naughty nun to gain her freedom from a daily existence she had found intolerable, was one of revenge against her uncle, who had angered him over a property dispute. He aimed to retaliate by putting forward Elizabeth's claim to the Lutton lands at Knapton, near Yedingham, but could not do so while she was out of circulation in the convent. Whatever the outcome, Constable's actions had surely proved more than satisfactory already from her point of view.

Other nuns at Yedingham with Elizabeth Lutton had been even younger than fifteen when they were fully professed. Dame Agnes Butterfield, for instance, was only twelve years old. She was in her late forties when the priory was suppressed in 1539 and like the other nuns there, she was described as being 'of good living'. Yet four years earlier, the King's notorious visitors to all the religious houses had named her amongst nuns who had given birth. Such a difference of personal descriptions even befell seventy year old Dame Alice Brampton of Handale Priory, on the north-east coast of Yorkshire, although she was long past childbearing age.

The last prioress of Handale was Alice Lutton, an older kinswoman of the abducted Elizabeth, and another member of the family, Mary, was listed amongst the servants as a butler there. The words 'Continue', 'Continue in religion' or 'Religion' were written beside the names of the nuns of Handale, Yedingham and various nunneries throughout Yorkshire, thereby stating that these women wished to remain bound by their religious vows – a situation which applied to the great majority of the county's nuns, in spite of the instances of scandal amongst them.

Under the 1536 Act of Suppression, to close smaller religious houses, all the Yorkshire nunneries were liable for closure. However, so many nuns wanted to transfer to another priory if theirs fell, that most houses were granted exemption, for the practical purpose of giving accommodation to displaced nuns. Unlike monks and canons, who could leave life in the cloisters for employment in the Church or the secular world, the nuns faced the limited opportunities which beset all Tudor women. Their main alternative to convent life was that of returning to the families who had put them in a nunnery, sometimes to be rid of them, and might not welcome them back! For elderly nuns such as Joan Scott, formerly the Prioress of Handale and 'aged ninety and blynde', the world outside their priory must have seemed like a foreign country – and a very frightening one too, especially for those who had spent most of their lives within the familiar surroundings of the nunnery, where they had thought they would end their days.

The nuns of vales and dales included all age groups from teenagers to nonagenarians. About a third of them, the largest age group, were in their forties and they provided most of the prioresses. The second largest group was that of nuns aged under thirty: they numbered about a quarter, so maybe the religious life had retained some appeal for younger women, at least in this county, as it had in bygone times.

The surnames of nuns in Yorkshire indicates that the priories sometimes recruited too from further afield, where nunneries were fewer. At Esholt Priory, for instance, Dame Agnes Cockayne came from a gentry family of Derbyshire, a county which had only one small nunnery. Two of Marrick Priory's nuns, Eleanor Maxwell and Grace Rutherford, and also Elizabeth Davison, listed as a pregnant nun of Nun Monkton Priory, were amongst several in Yorkshire who haled from Scottish Border families noted for their raiding in Tudor times. In contrast, another Marrick nun, also called Elizabeth, had the Yorkshire surname, Close. And yet another Elizabeth belonged to the northern, noble Percy family, but may have come from a junior branch, for she was the youngest nun at Wykeham Priory, near the coastal village of Seamer, where they lived. When her prioress,

Dame Katherine Nandyke, took office in 1508, Elizabeth Percy was not yet born. This long-serving prioress had her own separate chamber 'hard by the churche' for over thirty years, and a female relative, Isabel Nandyke – probably her niece – was amongst the Wykeham nuns.

Members of the same families were together at other Yorkshire nunneries too and possibly included twins: Alice and Anne Peacock of Yedingham were both listed as aged twenty-nine when the priory was closed. The distinctly northern-sounding surname of Sedgwick turned up near the county's south-east coast, at Nunkeeling Priory, which housed Margaret and Alice from that family and also an Alice Tomlinson, who had relatives called Dorothy at nearby Swine Priory, as well as elderly Agnes further up the coast at Wykeham. Although none of Yorkshire's nunneries could boast of a nun with the appropriate surname of York, there was a Joan Lancaster at Watton Priory in this south-east corner of the county. Two women from the area's leading gentry family, the Ellerkers, were nuns here – Anne (the sub-prioress) and Agnes.

As for south-west Yorkshire, Prioress Isabel Arthington of Hampole nunnery, near Doncaster, shared the same surname as one of her own nuns, Elizabeth, and one called Agnes at Nun Appleton. Agnes Arthington's community of nuns also included two nuns related to each other – Margaret and Elizabeth Carter.

From 1536 onwards, Nun Appleton Priory took in extra nuns from the groups disbanded as other priories closed. In a few years to come, its new secular owners would be the couple involved in the romantic abduction from there in 1518 – Isabel and William Fairfax! But in the meantime, this family's further connection with Nun Appleton occurred with the arrival of Dame Jane Fairfax, who transferred here with a nun called Alice Sheffield when their priory at Sinningthwaite, about eight miles upstream near the river Wharfe, was dissolved. A year later, they were joined by Agnes Aislaby and Elizabeth Parker from the former Ellerton-on-Swale Priory, near Richmond.

Curiously, the family name of one of the other nuns from there was the same as the river which flowed past this nunnery - Cecilia Swale. However, she led an unsettled life while she was at Ellerton: there were reports that she had a child and then sought release from her religious vows, but she had a change of heart and accepted a transfer across the county to the largest Yorkshire nunnery at Swine Priory. She was in the company of a resident mother-nun there, Elizabeth Copelay, whose child had been fathered by a priest.

Some of the nunneries singled out for closure in 1536 owned shrines and relics believed to be of special benefit for women. Perhaps some tradition rooted in ancient folklore, that St Bridget was a Christian version of the Celtic earth-mother goddess, Brigantia, had influenced pilgrimages to Arden Priory in the North Yorkshire Moors. Women made offerings to 'the image of St Brigett' there 'for cows lost and ill'. From the late summer of that year, however, they could no longer do so. Nor could they go on pilgrimage to the shrine of the patron saint of domestic servants, St Sitha, at Clementhorpe Priory in York, though they could still visit the similar shrine further east at Wykeham Priory – for the time being. A relic of the Virgin Mary's milk was not available any more either at Clementhorpe, but that at Basedale could still be used. Other childbirth aids which were put out of existence by the closures were the relics of St Margaret's arm and St Bernard's tunic at Sinningthwaite, St Stephen's finger and a piece of the Holy Cross at Keldholme and another piece of this at Nunburnholme Priory, near Pocklington in East Yorkshire. Only a third piece, several miles away at Nunkeeling, remained to provide possible comfort.

Nunburnholme was the poorest of the Yorkshire nunneries. Its 'Nun's Walk' still exists in the sheltered, wooded valley of the Yorkshire Wolds, where it stood by a stream called the Beck. A route through Deepdale led to a monastery about two miles away at Warter Priory, which was also dissolved in 1536. One of the canons there was

Ruins of Nunkeeling Priory

alleged to have committed 'incest with a nun', but no
indication was given regarding whether this was a sister
from his own family or a sister in the spiritual sense, from a
convent such as Nunburnholme. The closure of two
religious houses so near together was very unpopular in the
surrounding area and contributed to the strong local
support for the Pilgrimage of Grace rebellion in the early
autumn. Within two months of Nunburnholme being
dissolved, the parish rector, Richard Hawcliffe, and people
from the neighbourhood led Prioress Elizabeth Kilbourne
and her five nuns back along the Nun's Walk and, as the
new owner William Hungate later complained, 'put in
possession again the late suppressed prioress' at the former
priory.

Around the same time, in woodland near Arden Priory, a
spring still called the 'Nun's Well' briefly lived up to its
name again when the nuns were restored there by the rebels.
Sinningthwaite and Clementhorpe were also re-occupied by
their nuns during the rebellion. The rebel leader, Robert
Aske, later asserted that this happened because 'the
commons would needs put them in'. But a garbled, third-

hand report which reached the King and Court at Windsor Castle phrased matters very differently indeed. In this, the rebels who called themselves 'Pilgrims' were clearly blamed for the restoration of Clementhorpe nunnery and denounced as 'those knaves which now be up in Yorkshire'.

The informant of such news was stated to be 'one Mistress Beckwith', a gentlewoman 'who had escaped from them'. She may have been Elizabeth, the wife of Leonard Beckwith, the King's receiver of former monastic property in Yorkshire. He had been granted Holy Trinity Priory in York, when it was suppressed along with Clementhorpe nunnery, but he fled from the city at once when the rebels arrived there in mid-October 1536. The new secular owner of Clementhorpe, William Maunsell, another local official, stayed behind, but he complained subsequently that he had feared for his life.

Maunsell had taken up residence at Clementhorpe immediately after the nuns' departure. Tudor York, however, had been the scene of a riot against its closure before its four centuries of existence were ended so abruptly. To many of the citizens, the rebels converging on them from different areas of Yorkshire were welcome. Robert Aske had notices put on the great medieval Minster's doors, ordering the Clementhorpe nuns and Holy Trinity monks to resume life in their priories, and tales were told of this order being implemented during a torchlit procession amid cheering crowds.

Despite the prevailing atmosphere of rejoicing, though, one prominent resident of York was noted for her reluctance to re-enter the Clementhorpe cloisters. Prioress Isabel Ward had good reason to feel so unwilling, for she faced the dilemma of her own hopes for her priory being jeopardized by any association with the actions of rebels. She had endeavoured to save Clementhorpe by the more lawful means of appealing to Queen Jane Seymour for help. More details of her efforts were given in the report which mentioned Mistress Beckwith. Prioress Isabel offered 300 marks 'to the Queen's Grace' for such help and the money could be conveyed to Court by her brother-in-law, who was a member of the Ellerker family. He had requested a Lincolnshire gentleman named Christopher Ascue, who was then at Court, 'to move that matter to the Queen's Council, and to offer them money, and the abbess herself promised him £30 for his labor'. Ascue related this information in 'the Queen's Chamber at Windsor Castle', where Jane Seymour's Chancellor and Secretary 'promised to move the Queen'. He repeated the 'same tale to Margery Horsman, the Queen's gentlewoman'.

With the outbreak of rebellion, however, Ascue also received the extra 'news by a servant of his', Harry Sais, about the rebels' restoration of Clementhorpe, and he passed this on to Jane's Chancellor. Sais, who had been in York on business for his master, had left there with Mistress Beckwith and was threatened by rebels on the journey along the Great North Road, near the besieged Castle at Pontefract, before he accompanied this lady safely to the south.

Queen Jane was certainly 'moved' by the plight of the dissolved priories, but as shown in Chapter 2, she could not move the King on their behalf when she tried to plead with him in late October. The situation in Yorkshire was still volatile when the Pilgrimage of Grace ended in December and the restored nuns left their old priories for the very last time. The King did not proceed with any punishment against them and the prioresses each received their pensions. Isabel Ward retired to a house in nearby Trinity Lane in York for the remaining thirty-three years of her life. Her new home once belonged to Holy Trinity Priory and has been preserved as one of the city's finest medieval buildings, known as 'Jacob's Well', because it later became an inn with this name.

The last Prioress of Clementhorpe had succeeded to her office when she was only twenty-one years old. She was thirty-nine when the nunnery was dissolved, and she remained a devout Catholic at heart, in spite of all the religious changes during her lifetime. Her long retirement was probably a private version of the daily prayers and

Isabel Ward's home, Jacob's Well, York

devotions so familiar to her – and mostly peaceful, though she had the chance to observe some historic events, such as the execution of Robert Aske in 1537 and the visit by Henry VIII to York during his northern progress in 1541.

Near Robert Aske's family home at Aughton in the Vale of York, the nuns of Thicket Priory, headed by Prioress Agnes Beckwith, must have believed that their exemption from closure in 1536 would be permanent. They had a new kitchen and parlour built and also a 'woodehouse' with a room above, where the floorboarding was 'not yet fynysshid' when the priory was suppressed in August 1539. With the variations in Tudor spelling, Thicket has sometimes been referred to in documents as 'Thikhede', 'Tykehead' or 'Thickhead', but under whatever name, its fate came in the same month as six of the other Yorkshire nunneries were dissolved: nearby Wilberfoss Priory, Yedingham, Wykeham, Handale, Basedale and Esholt. In September, a commissioner called Sir John Uvedale closed Swine and Nunkeeling on consecutive days, then travelled to the other side of the county and dealt with Marrick Priory in the same way, about a week later, so that he could move into his new residence there. H.F.M. Prescott's novel, *The Man on a Donkey*, shows a small victory for the nuns, who had a final breakfast together before Uvedale arrived, but left the clearing up still to be done!

Only five Yorkshire nunneries then remained in existence. Four of them were in West Yorkshire and they survived for two more months until a spate of closures in this part of the county in the late autumn of 1539. Remarkably, Hampole was the only one dissolved before the large abbeys of Fountains and Kirkstall. A small nunnery in Calderdale, at Kirklees Priory, near Huddersfield, and Arthington and Nun Appleton all formally surrendered afterwards. Finally came the demise of Watton, during a further round of closures of East Yorkshire abbeys and priories.

In folklore and legend, Kirklees Priory has a claim to fame as the place where Robin Hood died and was buried. *A Lytell Geste of Robyn Hode* was first printed during the reign of Henry VII and referred to a medieval 'prioresse of

Kirkesley', his 'wicket' kinswoman whose medical treatment of him by blood-letting was blamed for his death. The last prioress, Dame Joan Kyppes, or Kippax, was no angel either, according to one report in 1535, which named her as pregnant, but this allegation was possibly a mistake and the name of one of her nuns should have been noted instead - that of Isabella Rhodes, who merited the comment of 'criminosus' in another report! One of the properties owned by the priory was the rectory at nearby Mirfield, where a house later nicknamed 'Papist Hall' became the home of the prioress and four of the seven Kirklees nuns in retirement. Here, the little community continued with a religious life together for many years. Isabella Rhodes and three other nuns – Isabel Hopton, Agnes Brooke and Isabel Saltonstall, each had relatives living nearby. The former prioress died in 1562 and was buried at Mirfield Church, where an inscription commemorates 'Dame Joan Kepast, late nun at Kirklees'. The youngest member of her priory, Isabel Saltonstall, was still alive and called 'the nun' by local folk almost forty years after Kirklees was closed. She managed to continue the saga of the naughtier nuns of vales and dales from bygone times, for she gained notoriety for being an old battleaxe and was involved in a court case in 1577 over a dispute with her neighbours.

One of the youngest nuns at Arthington Priory was also called Isabel and she too lived into old age. Dame Isabel Whitehead lived in the household of a Lady Middleton until this lady died, and then she stayed with a mother and daughter from the Yorkshire family which had been founders and patrons of her former nunnery – the Arthingtons. They remained Catholic throughout the Tudor period, but Dame Isabel and her two hostesses unfortunately became victims of the times, when their house was raided during the autumn of 1587 in a search for Catholic priests. The old ex-nun was threatened with drawn swords even though she lay ill. She and both the Arthington ladies were arrested and imprisoned in York Castle, where she died a few months later.

Although only fragments of details have survived about other former nuns of vales and dales in retirement, contemporary legal documents such as court records, wills and pension lists reveal occasional glimpses of some of them for half a century or more after the Pilgrimage of Grace. Three nuns of Moxby Priory, who did not transfer to other Yorkshire nunneries in 1536, for instance, each experienced very different lives afterwards. Frail, elderly Elizabeth Ward had been granted a lifelong form of annuity called a corrody by the prioress there, Philippa Jennison, but when Moxby was dissolved, the old nun received a lump sum instead of this and the money was handed over to an 'honest man', who undertook to look after her from then onwards.

Like Elizabeth Ward, Margaret Basford had no twice-yearly pension to support her. But despite the lack of information about how she fared for numerous years without financial provision, her story is one of the most clearly documented of the former nuns. Margaret was only twenty in 1536 and had been a nun since she was fourteen. She should therefore have been released from all her religious vows, on the two-fold grounds of the injunction freeing all those under the age of twenty-four and those professed as nuns before they were twenty. She married a man called Roger Newstead in 1549, partly for financial security as she later admitted.

In 1554, however, Margaret appeared before the Archbishop of York's court, accused of breaking her nun's vow of chastity by marrying. Times had suddenly changed from the Protestant reign of King Edward VI to the return of Roman Catholicism under Queen Mary Tudor, which brought the ending of priests' marriages – and those of ex-nuns too. Margaret was ordered to separate from her husband and resume wearing her nun's habit. She was forbidden from contact with Roger, except in public places such as the church and in the presence of witnesses. Once again, she was left without any income. Maybe her husband continued to pay for her maintenance secretly, with the help of go-betweens. Whatever informal arrangements there may have been, Margaret's life improved when Elizabeth I became Queen. The ex-nun returned to her husband and they were still together almost thirty years later, when she re-emerged briefly in the records as a witness in a 1586 court case. Another witness then was a former nun at Moxby with her, Elizabeth Burnett, who had somehow survived all those years as a single woman, without either pension or employment, yet stated that she had an income of at least forty shillings.

Whether the retired nuns were pensionless or pensioned, gifts or bequests of money were no doubt welcome. Sometimes these occurred because of the nuns keeping in touch with each other, an example being that of Dame Katherine Nandyke bequeathing money to all 'eight of my susters' who had been at Wykeham Priory with her. When she died in 1541, she gave extra items of silk and silver to the Wykeham 'suster' who was also 'Isabell Nandyke, my nece'. Cecilia Swale, the alleged naughty nun who transferred to Swine Priory in 1537, was amongst four nuns who received small bequests in 1550 from the former prioress of their first nunnery at Ellerton-on-Swale – Dame

Swine Priory Church

103

Joan Harkay. The others included Agnes Aislaby, who married a priest after the closure of her second convent, Nun Appleton.

Of the twenty nuns at Swine Priory when it was dissolved, no less than nine were named Elizabeth. Tudor records contained varied snippets about six of them afterwards: Elizabeth Thorne went to live in Hull, accompanied by Elizabeth Patricke, to whom she later bequeathed her house there. Elizabeth Grimston married 'oon Pikkerd' from the nearby village of Welwick. Elizabeth Tyas, whose family were connected with south-west Yorkshire, also married – her husband was 'John Swine, gentleman' of Tickhill, near Rotherham. Elizabeth Elsley was mentioned in the 1553 pension list as remaining with 'master Barton of Northallerton' in the north of the county. Elizabeth Clifton, however, was stated then to have sold her pension. The unnamed buyer certainly benefited from being able to receive her pension payments, for she was one of the ex-nuns still alive twenty years later! Mystery surrounds the amount of the purchase price, and how Elizabeth Clifton subsequently supported herself, but a likely source of help was her well-off Midlands family. Elizabeth Grimston and the last prioress, Dorothy Knight, were amongst the five nuns of Swine whose names appeared on the ever-dwindling pension list in 1573.

Some family wills included ex-nuns who returned home and were later remembered by a variety of relatives, such as the father of Isabel Norman of Handale Priory, the widowed mother of Isabel Craik of Wilberfoss, the brother-in-law of Agnes Aunger of Nun Appleton and even the sister's father-in-law of Joan Redman of Nun Monkton.

Queen Mary may have hoped that if any region of her realm would follow her example of reviving some abbeys and priories around London, Yorkshire would be true to its local name of 'God's own county'. If so, she was to be disappointed. But in 1686 – 150 years after Clementhorpe nunnery in York was dissolved – another Catholic monarch, King James II, reigned and a nunnery called the Bar Convent was established in the city, close to the site of Clementhorpe. The nuns belonged to the Institute of the Blessed Virgin Mary, a religious order which was founded overseas by a Yorkshirewoman from the same family as Prioress Isabel Ward, and a portrait of their foundress, Mary Ward, is displayed at the Bar Convent. These later Yorkshire nuns had to wait until the law of Catholic emancipation was passed in 1829 before they could safely wear religious habits in public, but nowadays their world-wide organization has expanded far beyond the county's vales and dales.

CHAPTER 7

The Belles of Shoreditch

The old nursery rhyme, *Oranges and Lemons,* with its line, 'When I grow rich, said the bells of Shoreditch', may seem to have little connection with Tudor women. Queen Elizabeth I, however, much enjoyed hearing the bells of St Leonard's Church, Shoreditch, pealing out when she passed by on her many royal progresses.

During the last decade of Elizabeth's long reign, the 1590s, a most unusual monument in tribute to a Tudor female ancestry was erected inside this church, with effigies of four ladies only, although its long epitaph also mentions two male relatives buried with them. From the birth of the oldest lady in the late 15th century, to the death of the youngest of this foursome in the late 16th, the three generations commemorated here have a combined lifespan which was entirely within the Tudor period. They came from the east, the west and the north of the realm, but they all died in the south, at the site of a former nunnery near Shoreditch Church.

As the epitaph says, this monument resulted from an all-female initiative, being 'founded by the lady Adeline Nevel, at the direction of … lady Katharine Constable, deceased, her sister, in February 1591.' Katharine left money in her will to cover the cost of the memorial which includes her own effigy along with those of both her grandmothers – the Countesses of Westmorland and Rutland - and her aunt Margaret, who was the daughter and daughter-in-law of these and became the 2nd Countess of Rutland. All three seem to have formed a lasting friendship within their close family ties, despite the irresponsible behaviour of some of their menfolk, and perhaps because grandmother Lady Westmorland was also Katharine's godmother, these ladies' approach of mutual support had a beneficial effect, both on herself and her sister Adeline.

Monument to four Tudor ladies in Shoreditch Church, London

Shoreditch was still surrounded by green fields when it provided the setting for the formal beginning of the kinship between the Westmorland and Rutland families. Here, 'beside London, in the Erle of Ruttlandes place' near the Benedictine nunnery of Holywell, or Halliwell, an elaborate triple wedding was celebrated on Monday 3rd July 1536 as the social event of that turbulent year. The Tudor chronicler, Charles Wriothesley, described it as 'a greate solempnytie of marriage' between the Westmorlands' heir, Lord Henry Neville and the Rutlands' eldest daughter, Lady Anne Manners; the Rutlands' heir, Lord Henry, and the Westmorlands' daughter, Lady Margaret; and their eldest daughter, Lady Dorothy Neville, and the Earl of Oxford's heir, John de Vere. 'All the greate estates of the realme, both lordes and ladyes' were present. The wedding ceremony took place in the large chapel of Holywell Priory, and in the procession 'after masse' en route to the 'greate dynner', Lady Anne (the future mother of Katharine and Adeline Neville) was led out by the Duke of Suffolk and Marquis of Dorset. Lady Margaret – whose effigy would one day be amongst the four kneeling at a prayer desk on the Shoreditch tomb – was led by her cousin, the Earl of Surrey and a distant kinsman, the Earl of Derby.

King Henry VIII turned up 'in a maske' with '11 more with him'. They all 'daunsed with the ladies a good while' and then the King took off his mask, added to his state of obesity by eating 'a great bankett of 40 dishes' and returned to his palace once 'the bankett ended'.

The oldest of the Shoreditch ladies, Countess Eleanor of Rutland, was described as 'a wondrous good lady'. She was born around 1497 into the Paston family of Norfolk, who were famous for their letters during the 15th-century Wars of the Roses and into the early Tudor period. The Paston women were generally rather tough and determined, but Eleanor's grandmother, Margery Brews, was noted for her more pleasant nature and some of this may have come out in Eleanor. Margery's marriage to John Paston was a love-match and some of the letters to him were love letters, including Valentine messages. Even so, Margery did not neglect to observe her expected demeanour of subservience to her husband and began her letters by addressing him as 'Right reverend and worshipful sir'!

Eleanor and her husband, Thomas Manners, 1st Earl of Rutland, were both much respected members of the royal household and despite her numerous pregnancies, she made a successful career at Court as a senior lady-in-waiting to most of Henry VIII's wives. One time when she was in attendance on his fourth wife, Anna of Cleves, Countess Eleanor stepped into the limelight of history in a scene when Queen Anna's answers to some polite enquiries from her ladies indicated that the royal marriage had not been consummated. The Queen told them of the late night and early morning kisses she received from the King and seemed dismayed to hear from Eleanor that this was 'not enough' and 'more' was needed to make her with child. Soon, Queen Anna staved off any more personal questions by hinting that the King's present levels of attention towards her were quite enough for her! She enjoyed her freedom to the utmost after the six-month, unconsummated marriage ended with an amicable divorce.

The Earl of Rutland praised his wife for her generosity and affection towards their children. Her duties at the Tudor Court, however, meant that she needed to rely on family members and servants to take charge of their care and the running of the Rutlands' houses and lands. Her times at home were more likely to be at Holywell than at the ancestral home at Belvoir Castle, Leicestershire. Early in King Henry's reign, Dame Thomasine Percival (see Chapter 3) had been a benefactress of the old nunnery at Shoreditch, but when it was dissolved in 1539, the Rutlands took over its site to enlarge their London residence.

Their third son, Roger Manners, followed his mother's example by establishing a career at Court, where he served as 'Esquire to the Body' in the households of both Queens Mary and Elizabeth. He wrote frequently to the second son, John, famed in Tudor romance for his love-match with Dorothy Vernon of Haddon Hall in Derbyshire (her story is told in *Tales of Tudor Women*). The fourth and fifth sons, Thomas and Oliver Manners, are the two kinsmen mentioned on the Shoreditch epitaph, which refers to their 'valour' and 'valiant services' on military campaigns. But although this tomb was such a female venture, no mention is made of the courage shown by one of the ladies, Countess Katherine of Westmorland, against northern rebels during the Pilgrimage of Grace.

A contemporary report acknowledged, however, that she 'rather playeth the part of a knight than a lady'. She had not sought to be in a perilous situation at her home, Brancepath Castle in County Durham, but such an occurrence came about because 'the absence of the Bishop of Durham and the Earl of Westmorland sets all this country out of order. My lady of Westmorland, with the counsel she takes, stays the country for the time …' The Countess herself wrote to her husband amid the crisis as 'she that would be glad to hear from you, as I never heard since you went to London …' His lordship had in fact fled even further south to visit an uncle in Hampshire. He had heard a rumour that he was to be made a warden in the Border Country with Scotland and he betook himself away from the north to try and prevent this appointment, for which he admitted feeling 'diffident of his capacity for the office'.

The Earl certainly had no diffidence in his capacity to make his wife frequently pregnant, in which condition she probably was at the time she refused to be intimidated by the rebels. When the Bailiff of Durham brought a messenger with a letter to her from their leaders, Countess Katherine took prompt and vigorous action: the messenger was detained in her custody and she ordered the arrest of any others who might come. She thanked the Bailiff and immediately sent a copy of the letter to her husband, telling him to show it to the Lord Privy Seal, Thomas Cromwell. 'I keep the original,' she added efficiently, before appealing to him to return home. The townsfolk of Durham, meanwhile, seized their Bailiff and threatened to behead him if the messenger was not released, so he was obliged to obtain the man's freedom from the Countess's custody.

The Shoreditch epitaph tells very briefly of this resolute lady's background. Born in Wales into the powerful Stafford family, she was 'daughter to Edward, Duke of Buckingham', who was descended from the 14th-century king, Edward III, and was regarded as a potential rival to the Tudors for the throne. Henry VIII had him beheaded for treason. The Earl of Westmorland was one of the Duke's wards, and Lady Katherine Stafford may have been a second choice of wife for him. Her equally strong-willed sister, Elizabeth, claimed that their father 'had bought my Lord Westmorland for me; and he and I loved together for two years, and had not my Lord, my husband, made suit for me after his first wife's death, I had married my Lord Westmorland …' She complained about her husband, the Duke of Norfolk, and his ill-treatment of her because she 'would not suffer' his 'bawd and harlots in the house'. 'The bawd' was the Duke's mistress, Bess Holland, and she and some 'drabs' were once alleged to have bound Duchess Elizabeth and sat on her breasts until she 'spat blood'.

A Neville family guest at that Holywell triple wedding was the wife of Lord Westmorland's cousin, Lord Latimer. Her name was Katherine Parr, and at the same time as the Countess of Westmorland stood up to rebels, young Lady Latimer and her two stepchildren were in similar danger. Their home at Snape Hall in North Yorkshire was surrounded by a mob of rebels during her husband's absence in London. Her attempts to negotiate with them failed, and under threats of violence, she found little option but to let them into the house, though she managed to send a message to her husband to rescue her and the children. After he succeeded in doing so, she took her turn to save his life, for he had reluctantly taken part in the Pilgrimage of Grace because of threats to his family. The need to explain his involvement to the King was especially great, in view of the fact that Lord Latimer had an enemy in the much-hated Thomas Cromwell, who was in the process of arresting other Pilgrimage leaders.

Katherine Parr's royal connections were not those of ancestry, like Countess Katherine's, but those of the Parr family, whose service and loyalty to the Tudors had been strong through two generations. Her natural prudence and discretion had not worked in her dealings with a mob of rebels at Snape Hall, but these qualities helped her with the tyrant King. Katherine Parr had been brought up and educated with his daughter, Mary, when her mother, Lady Maud Parr, was a lady-in-waiting to Queen Katharine of Aragon, so she was able to gain the daunting experience of a personal interview with Henry VIII. She gently explained to him about her own and Lord Latimer's endeavours to further the royal cause amongst the rebels, despite the intimidation they suffered, and she offered a vivid eye-witness account of their experiences under such duress. The

King, knowing her sincerity and the Parrs' undoubted loyalty, stopped Cromwell from proceeding against her husband.

Six years later, Lord Latimer died from illness and his widow became the new Queen through her rather reluctant marriage to King Henry in July 1543. Her stepdaughter, Margaret Neville, was appointed to her household and Countess Eleanor of Rutland remained at Court as one of her ladies.

Eleanor continued to serve in this role after she was widowed herself in the autumn of that year, but as before, she spent time at Holywell too. When the 'Lady Margeret Nevell', commemorated with her on the Shoreditch tomb, became the new Countess of Rutland and so took charge of the household at Holywell, the Rutlands' residence there went on welcoming guests from both the Manners and Neville families. Countess Margaret and her mother and mother-in-law Countesses had much in common for a friendship to grow between them during their times of social contact at Holywell. They had Court gossip and goings-on to talk about, for instance, in addition to all the matters concerned with their extensive families – including a murder plot hatched in their very midst.

The other Manners-Neville marriage from the Holywell triple wedding had proved to be unhappy. Lady Anne Manners was good and pious, but these qualities displeased one person in particular – her husband, Henry Neville. Their daughter, Katharine, was about five years old when Lord Henry was found guilty, in the autumn of 1546, of planning to use sorcery to murder his wife and father. He confessed from his prison that his gambling debts were so deep that he fell prey to an unscrupulous conman who claimed to be a magician. This man, Gregory Wilson, offered his services to solve his lordship's money problems by killing his father, Lord Westmorland, whom the gullible Henry Neville would then succeed as Earl. And while they were about such a drastic solution, why not also despatch Lady Anne soon to her eternal rest amongst other saints in heaven? Neville's confession saved him from execution and he was released after Henry VIII's death. One of his intended victims, his father, was then ordered to pay off his gambling debts. At the time of this plot, his wife may already have been pregnant with the Shoreditch tomb-builder, Lady Adeline, who was born in 1547.

Both the targets of the plot predeceased Lady Anne's mother, Countess Eleanor, who died at Holywell in 1551. Countess Katherine of Westmorland probably took her granddaughter-goddaughter, Katharine Neville, on visits to the close-knit family circle there from an early age. Katharine was ten years old when her other grandmother Eleanor died, fourteen when Countess Katherine died in May 1555 and eighteen when her aunt, Countess Margaret, died in October 1559. No doubt she was amongst the 'many mornars' at the magnificent funerals recorded for each of these ladies 'at Soredyche', which involved much pageantry and the requisite 'gret dener' afterwards.

The personal visits to Holywell clearly continued for Katharine and Adeline Neville until they were middle-aged themselves. By then, many years had passed since their brother Charles, the 6th Earl of Westmorland, and two of their Neville uncles were amongst the leaders of the failed Northern Rising of 1569 against Queen Elizabeth.

On the Manners side of their family, the next Lady Rutland after Countess Margaret was a close friend of Queen Elizabeth – Bridget Hussey, whose father had been implicated in rebelling against Henry VIII a few months after attending that 1536 Shoreditch wedding. (The strange story of her sister is told in the next chapter).

Katharine Neville herself married a kinsman of her two stepmothers, 'Sir John Constable of Holderness', as her epitaph says of this Yorkshire knight. She was a widow for twelve years, before she died at Holywell in 1591 and soon shared her Shoreditch memorial with her other 'right honourable and noble ladies'.

Even then, however, Tudor history was not quite over for the descendants of those Manners-Neville weddings at

Shoreditch. Katharine and Adeline had a niece called Margaret Neville who had been an infant when their brother Charles, her father, led the Northern Rising and fled into exile. Margaret was brought up a Catholic, but in 1594, she was found harbouring a priest, for which she was tried at Durham Assizes and sentenced to death. While she was awaiting execution, she was placed in the custody of Bishop Hutton of Durham, later Archbishop of York. Under his guidance, she renounced her faith and was then reprieved.

After granting a pardon to this Margaret Neville, Queen Elizabeth continued enjoying the peal of those Shoreditch Church bells for almost another decade before her own demise in 1603.

CHAPTER 8

A Reversal of Fortune

'Poor women of the country, of their charity, knowing my Lord's demayne always to his wives, brought me to my great window in the night such meat or drink as they had, and gave me, for the love of God; for money I had none wherewith to pay them, nor yet have had of my Lord, these four years, four groats.'

Lady Elizabeth Hungerford acknowledged in a letter of petition to the Lord Privy Seal, Thomas Cromwell, in 1540 that she would have died 'long ago' without the help of poor women from the area around her home at Farleigh Hungerford Castle in Somerset. The irony was that she had become a noble baroness during Whitsun week of 1536, when her husband, Lord Walter Hungerford, was raised to the peerage with the title, 1st Baron Hungerford of Heytesbury, in Wiltshire. The great lady of a local area would usually take up the duty of being 'Lady Bountiful' to give alms to the poorest of her neighbours, but at Farleigh Hungerford, the castle ruins still include a tower which was the scene of Lord Hungerford's 'demayne' towards Elizabeth, his third wife.

'Here I have byn these three or fower yeares past,' she told Cromwell, 'without comfort of any creature, and under the custodie of my Lord's chaplain, Sir John a Lee, which once or twice poyson'd me, as he will not deny upon examination'. When this priest heard that Cromwell ordered her husband to give her a yearly allowance, he 'promised my Lord that he would soon rid him of me, and I am sure he intendeth to keep that promise'. She feared more each day to taste the meat and drink he provided for her, which was brought to her by her husband's 'foole'. Her letter contained such harrowing descriptions as 'lacke of sustenance' and 'well nigh starved', as well as her admission that 'sometime, for lack of water, saving your honour and reverence,' that she resorted to drinking 'mine owne water'.

Elizabeth added that she had 'no earthly friend' but Cromwell 'able to help' her. She knew that other people had not dared to do so 'for fear of my Lord's displeasure'. Her petition was for release from her close prison and also divorce, because instead of continuing 'this wretched life' with her husband, she preferred to destroy herself or beg her living from door to door. She hinted darkly that she would perish soon, unless Cromwell commanded her husband to bring her and the chaplain before him, and then he would 'find out many strange things' about Lord Hungerford!

The first part of her wish came true shortly after her letter, though not in the way she expected. The second part – to be divorced – was no longer necessary by that time, as she was a widow when her captivity ended. Her husband's head was already 'sett on London Bridge' as that of a traitor and his body 'buried within the Tower of London'. Some of those 'strange things' about him had become wider known and led to his execution, on the same July day in 1540 as Cromwell himself was beheaded for treason.

Lord Hungerford was condemned, not for imprisoning his wife, but as contemporary chronicler Charles Wriothesley stated, 'for treason of boggery', raping his daughter and 'having practised magic and invocation of devils' to predict the date of King Henry VIII's death. Witnesses of his beheading said that at his death, he 'seemed so unquiet that many judged him to be rather frenzied than otherwise'.

A further consequence of Hungerford's execution was the passing of a law, which made foretelling the King's death a crime of high treason. Even when Henry VIII was on his own death-bed in 1547, his physicians were too afraid to tell him.

A decade earlier, however, during Lady Elizabeth's captivity at Farleigh Hungerford, her parents and future father-in-law all suffered imprisonment in the Tower of

London, for very varied reasons. Her elderly father, Lord Hussey, was beheaded at Lincoln in 1537 for his part, during the previous autumn, in the failed Lincolnshire Rebellion (mentioned in Chapter 1). Her mother, Lady Anne, was arrested and questioned for inadvertently referring 'of custom' to the King's older daughter as 'the Princess'. (Mary Tudor had been demoted to the illegitimate 'Lady Mary' in 1533, after her parents' divorce). Both of Elizabeth Hungerford's parents had opposed the divorce from Katharine of Aragon. So too had her father-in-law-to-be, Sir George Throckmorton, who even warned King Henry against marrying Anne Boleyn, having 'already meddled with the mother and the sister'!

Coughton Court, Warwickshire

Sir George was head of the prolific Midlands family, whose main home was at Coughton Court, near Stratford-on-Avon in Warwickshire. He had the magnificent gatehouse built there, and was at odds with Thomas Cromwell over several matters, including a boundary dispute concerning a nearby property owned by the seemingly all-powerful Lord Privy Seal. Sir George's wife, Lady Katherine, was the mother of their eighteen children and also the aunt of three members of the Parr family, who were then in great favour with the King – Sir William Parr and his sisters, Katherine and Anne.

Katherine Parr's success in outmanoeuvring Cromwell and interceding with Henry to save her husband's life after the Pilgrimage of Grace (mentioned in Chapter 7) was repeated in 1540 to obtain her uncle George Throckmorton's release from the Tower. She was at Court for her sister's wedding to Sir William Herbert, and her remarkable qualities of tact and quiet diplomacy impressed the King so much again that he questioned Sir George about Cromwell. The combined efforts of uncle and niece provided some of the evidence which caused this notorious minister's downfall.

When the widowed Katherine became Queen in 1543, the Throckmortons rose in royal favour too - including their eldest son and heir, Sir Robert, and in a true reversal of fortune, his new second wife, the former Lady Elizabeth Hungerford. For the first ten years of this marriage, she was lady of the manor at the attractive village of Weston Underwood, near Olney in north Buckinghamshire. This had been acquired by the Throckmortons in the 15th century, through a marriage to an heiress. Lady Elizabeth would no longer have felt isolated within such a numerous family, which almost inevitably included several other Elizabeth Throckmortons. One of these was her stepdaughter, another was one of her own daughters, and on visits to Coughton Court, she probably gained occasional glimpses of her husband's aged great-aunt, the last Abbess of Denny Abbey in Cambridgeshire. The once powerful and influential

Abbess Elizabeth had returned to her ancestral home at Coughton, accompanied by two or three of her nuns, after the abbey was dissolved. They occupied an upper chamber, where they continued their religious life attired in their nuns' habits and mostly kept to their chamber, especially when the family had many visitors. Abbess Elizabeth died in January 1547, two weeks before the King. She was buried in Coughton Church, where a plaque on the end of a 19th-century tomb commemorates her.

Five years later, Sir George was also laid to rest there, and Sir Robert and Lady Elizabeth inherited Coughton Court. However, Elizabeth may not have had long to enjoy this as her main home, because some accounts give her date of death as January 1554, although others, including the *Lincolnshire Pedigrees*, state this to be 1571, the date of her brass memorial in Weston Underwood Church. A curious coincidence for a woman whose father and first husband were both beheaded, is that the figure of her, wearing an embroidered gown with slashed sleeves, was mentioned in old guidebooks as having the head missing. Nowadays her brass has a replica of the original head. Two of her daughters, also depicted on this memorial, married into leading Catholic families of nearby Northamptonshire: Anne Throckmorton married Sir William Catesby of Ashby St Ledger and Muriel married Sir Thomas Tresham of Rushton, who built the well-known Elizabethan folly called the Triangular Lodge.

Sir Thomas began another lodge, at Lyveden New Bield, near Oundle, but it was unfinished when he died and never completed, for his son and heir, Francis, was implicated in the Gunpowder Plot on 5th November 1605 and did not long outlive him. Anne's son, Robert Catesby, was the leader of the Plot, though his name is far less known in popular memory than that of his fellow-conspirator, Guy Fawkes.

When Lady Elizabeth, having survived her terrible ordeal at Farleigh Hungerford Castle, married into the Throckmorton family in 1542, the year when Mary Queen of Scots was born, she could never have envisaged that her sister, Bridget, would be the Chief Mourner at Mary's funeral, or that two of her own grandsons would be part of such a notorious plot to blow up Mary's son, King James I. Some of the plotters' wives were even in the upstairs room of the gatehouse at Coughton Court when Robert Catesby's servant, Robert Bates, came to tell them that the 'Gunpowder, Treason and Plot' had failed.

Triangular Lodge, Rushton, Northamptonshire

CHAPTER 9

The Wolf Women

Leicestershire legends tell that the tragic Nine-days' Queen of England, Lady Jane Grey, was attacked by a wolf while she was helping to rescue a small, injured child from its clutches. The wolf was said to be the last one ever encountered in Charnwood Forest, near Jane's Leicestershire home at Bradgate Park and was killed in a team effort by her and a neighbour's son.

Lady Jane Grey

Jane almost had a wolf-lady as her mother-in-law, but during the various struggles for power and supremacy in mid-Tudor times, she was married off elsewhere soon before her short reign in 1553. Her former betrothed eventually fell in love with her younger sister, Catherine, who gained a mother-in-law with a reputation as 'that Hell' instead! (Lady Catherine Grey's story is told in *Tales of Tudor Women*).

121

A small brass plate, dated 1604, in the nave of Eccleston Church, Lancashire, mentions the wolf-lady more respectfully. It commemorates 'William Dicconson, sometime stewarde over that most honourable householde of the high and mightie Princes Ann, Duches of Somerset'. High and 'mightie' she certainly was, but she was never a princess, even though she boasted of her descent from the medieval King Edward III. She was born around 1497, the daughter of a Suffolk knight, Sir Edward Stanhope of Sudbury. The wolf connection with her was two-fold, as it was the Stanhope family crest and Wolf Hall was the Wiltshire ancestral home of her husband, Sir Edward Seymour, elder brother of Queen Jane Seymour. Anne Stanhope was his second wife, his first – Katherine Fillol, having been consigned to a nunnery by him for adultery with his father.

Anne had served Queen Katharine of Aragon as a lady-in-waiting for several years and during these, she formed a lasting friendship with Mary Tudor, who called her affectionately 'my good Nann'. Mary thanked her wholeheartedly for her 'earnest gentleness' towards herself and also her retinue, a personal tribute which sheds pleasant light on an unattractive character generally known for being 'imperious'.

The formidable Anne has been identified as the lady symbolized by the beautiful, but 'coy' and 'froward' white Wolf in the Earl of Surrey's poem, *Of a Lady That Refused To Dance With Him*. Her pride and arrogance were such that she easily outmatched his own, when she snubbed him 'with spite and great disdain', telling him scornfully, 'Thou shall not play with me.' The Earl's over-reaction to her 'cruel' conduct led to most of his poem being an outpouring of angry, defiant vitriol against her and threats of violent revenge on others 'that never made offence'. His noble family, the Howards, regarded hers as upstarts.

The Seymours, though, had the satisfaction that *their* 'Jane the Quene' presented Henry VIII with his longed-for, legitimate male heir, Prince Edward, in October 1537. Soon after the baby's baptism, Edward Seymour was created Earl of Hertford. The patent for his new earldom provided that the title would descend to the male heirs of Anne Stanhope, but excluded Katherine Fillol's sons, who had been disinherited. A few days later, Queen Jane died of puerperal fever. The Seymour family's high place in the King's favour remained secure for the rest of his reign.

King Henry visited Wolf Hall in August 1539 – his second time there, and he was accompanied by about 200 members of his Court. Anne no doubt enjoyed the prestige of being hostess to such important guests, though Wolf Hall could hardly accommodate such a number. She and her husband, now themselves of noble status, were apparently obliged to stay in the adjacent Great Barn during the four-day visit! Their children were sent with her widowed mother-in-law, Dame Margery Seymour, to one of the forest lodges in nearby Savernake Forest.

The Great Barn, Wolf Hall, Wiltshire

When the King and Court descended upon Wolf Hall again in 1543, circumstances had changed rapidly since his previous visit. Having divorced his fourth wife and beheaded his fifth, he appeared to be enjoying the company of a circle of intelligent women, which included his daughter, Mary. Her friends, Anne Stanhope, Countess of Hertford, and the recently-widowed Katherine Parr, Lady

Latimer, belonged to this, along with Katherine's sister, Lady Anne Herbert, and close friend, Katherine, Duchess of Suffolk.

The corpulent monarch's wedding to Katherine Parr (mentioned in Chapters 7 and 8) was attended by all the rest of this group of ladies. Their mutual support and friendship helped her to survive in her unenviable new role as Henry VIII's sixth wife, which lasted for over three years. As a talented writer, she expressed her thoughts years later on her own view of this situation – her mind had been 'fully bent' to marry Sir Thomas Seymour 'before any man I know. Howbeit God withstood my will therein most vehemently for a time and ... made me renounce utterly mine own will, and to follow His will most willingly ...'

Anne Stanhope's view was also given with hindsight and, typically, she did not mince her words. She archly observed, "Did not Henry VIII marry Katherine Parr in his doting days, when he had brought himself so low by his lust and cruelty that no lady that stood on her honour would venture on him?" During the King's twilight years, however, the strong-minded Anne was more of a background figure who was loyal to her husband and also one of Queen Katherine's close circle of ladies. There were occasional glimpses of her, for instance, as 'my Lady of Hertford' was said to be one of the Queen's attendants who showed compassion towards a young Protestant woman and future martyr called Anne Askew, by sending money to her when she was imprisoned.

But there were signs too that Countess Anne was biding her time, awaiting circumstances when she would be rather like the Alpha-female in a wolf-pack and very much the first lady in the land. Her ambitions were tied in with those of her husband, who was easily commanded by her in private life. In 1544, she became anxious about him when he was away on military duties in the north, which involved implementing the King's ruthless orders for an invasion of Scotland, aptly-named in history as the 'Rough Wooing'. Anne sought help from Queen Katherine through their mutual friend, the Lady Mary, to speak to the King about recalling her husband to London. The Queen and her royal stepdaughter wrote jointly to reassure Anne that her request would be granted before Henry VIII set off for France to lead a military campaign there himself.

Countess Anne probably hoped that her husband would be appointed the Regent, who would rule the realm during the King's absence overseas – and this would be a rehearsal for taking on the powerful role completely when the infant, half-Seymour heir succeeded to the throne. To her dismay, he was chosen to be one of the support group of advisors when Queen Katherine Parr was entrusted with the regency, like Queen Katharine of Aragon in the early years of Henry VIII's reign. The sixth wife followed the example of the first wife in proving to be more than equal to the task.

A week before the old King's death in January 1547, the poet Earl of Surrey was beheaded. At the very outset of the new reign, the boy King Edward VI's uncle and aunt, the Earl and Countess of Hertford, promoted themselves to the higher rank of Duke and Duchess of Somerset. This reflected their new status, for at last their time of power seemed to have come when the Regent took the title of Lord Protector, or Protector Somerset. Katherine Parr was now the Dowager Queen, and no longer did Anne Stanhope, the wife who ruled the man who now ruled the kingdom, need to approach her for favours to be granted. The 'high and mightie' Anne, Duchess of Somerset, was the lady who received such requests instead! And so she did - one of them being from her own friend and King Edward's older sister, Lady Mary, who wrote to her 'good Nann' almost apologetically about 'troubling' her for help in securing pensions for faithful, long-term servants, 'for their years be so far passed, that I fear they shall not enjoy them for long'.

With no requirement whatsoever to be a proverbial 'wolf in sheep's clothing' in her approach any more, Anne targeted various people to attack. She humiliated the young King's tutor, Sir John Cheke, over a supposed misdemeanour by his wife, and had the audacity to reprove one of her husband's main supporters, Sir Thomas Smith, about his display of a notable fault of her own – haughtiness. Queen Katherine Parr wrote of Duchess Anne, 'it is her custom to promise many comings to her friends, and to perform none. I trust in greater matters she is more circumspect'. Unfortunately, this hope expressed by Katherine was not fulfilled and she herself became the prime victim of the wolf-lady's frustration.

Another of the Dowager Queen's hopes was achieved, however, when she secretly married Thomas Seymour a few months after Henry VIII's death. Sir Thomas was now the Lord High Admiral, but Duchess Anne prepared to pounce on the royal lady whose train-bearer she had been in her former days as an attendant. Anne decided that Katherine had forsaken her rights as Dowager Queen by marrying the younger Seymour brother, whose rank was so far beneath hers. "And shall I now give place to her," she stormed, as she derided Katherine. " ... If Master Admiral teach his wife no better manners, I am she that will."

Anne Stanhope's own manners were hardly exemplary, though, when she not only refused to bear Katherine's train at Court, but physically jostled and tried to push the startled Queen out of the leading position during Court entrances and exits. The Lord Protector's wife asserted that *she* now took precedence as first lady. She was most reluctant to accept that legally, she was not. The Act of Succession was clearly in Queen Katherine's favour in the order of precedence, with the other royal ladies, Mary, Elizabeth and Anna of Cleves all being ahead of Duchess Anne.

Opinions about Anne were generally in agreement that the Lord Protector had 'a bad wife'. She soon found a means of satisfying some of her unquenched thirst for power through a bitter dispute which developed over Katherine's jewellery. Anne claimed that personal gifts to Katherine from Henry VIII were Crown property. The usually mild-mannered Katherine was so outraged that she referred to Anne as 'that Hell' and even acknowledged, after an argument with the Protector, that if this had occurred during a face-to-face encounter, she would have vented her anger by biting him!

In September 1548, Anne moved up a place in the order of precedence when Queen Katherine died in childbirth. Her baby daughter was named after the Lady Mary and was also known as 'the Queen's child'. She was orphaned and disinherited at the tender age of seven months when her father, Thomas Seymour, was beheaded for treason. One of his last requests was that little Mary Seymour would be brought up by Katherine, Duchess of Suffolk. 'Some pension allotted' to the infant for her upkeep failed to appear, despite Duchess Katherine writing to 'my Lady of Somerset at large' on the matter. Meanwhile, 'my Lady of Suffolk' bore the whole costs of upkeep and was additionally faced with the child's servants daily calling 'for their wages, whose voices my ears hardly bear, but my coffers much worse'.

Protector Somerset fell from power in October 1549, so ending Anne's 'reign' after only two and a half years. The new regime soon helped Katherine, Duchess of Suffolk's coffers by restoring property to Mary Seymour, which provided the much-needed funds for her upbringing. Some mystery surrounds the fate of this 'Queen's child' after her second birthday, however, and she is believed to have died in infancy.

Duchess Anne was blamed as a major cause of her husband's downfall, because her high-handed ways alienated his friends as well as his foes. She was such a dominant character, but being a woman, she could only exercise her ambition and power through others – and even then, not as fully as she wished. Her conduct seems to reflect an element of deep exasperation with the reality of her limited situation.

The old saying that 'pride comes before a fall' was not entirely true in Anne's case, for though her pride certainly preceded her loss of power, it also continued afterwards. She was amongst the Seymour family members imprisoned in the Tower of London when her husband was arrested on charges of treason in October 1551. But if any noblewoman expected to continue in the luxurious lifestyle to which she had grown accustomed – even as a prisoner – it was this lady! She still wore velvet clothes and used napkins and various utensils of silver during her meals, in addition to providing for her daily needs with her own bed linen, towels, books and money. Even so, the price she paid for her loyalty to husband and family was a two-year period of captivity, during which she was widowed. Both her husband and her brother, Sir Michael Stanhope, were executed.

Duchess Anne was a prisoner in the Tower when Lady Jane Grey was also there, ruling for nine July days in 1553. Then one August day, a true friend arrived with all due ceremony at the Tower. A friend who still called the Duchess 'my good Nann', and greeted her amongst a group of kneeling prisoners, raised Anne to her feet, embraced her, and set her free from captivity - Mary Tudor, the new Queen of England. Soon, a royal residence fit for queens was granted to Anne for the rest of her life. Hanworth Manor in Middlesex had belonged to Anne Boleyn and Katherine Parr. Duchess Anne's time there lasted for thirty-four years, most of them with her second husband, Sergeant Francis Newdigate. He was a former Seymour official, who sometimes tended to be an interfering and disagreeable character, so this couple were probably well-matched!

Anne died in April 1587 at the great age of ninety and was buried in Westminster Abbey, where her monument is near the magnificent tombs of Tudor royalty. Some accounts of her say that she also has a memorial at Shelford Church, Nottinghamshire, which contains a worn effigy of a Lady Ann Stanhope, who died in 1587. However, this commemorates her sister-in-law, the wife of her executed brother, Sir Michael Stanhope, and the lady predeceased Duchess Anne by two months – dying in the same February as the captive Mary Queen of Scots.

Nottinghamshire's near neighbour, Derbyshire, provides an unusual link with a lady nicknamed the 'She-Wolf', who was born in 1540, only two years before the Queen of Scots.

Lettice Knollys was the daughter of Mary's early custodian, Sir Francis Knollys. Both ladies were amongst the many visitors who took the waters at Buxton in Elizabethan times and made their mark by including 'thinges' in the various items of graffiti engraved on windows of the 'goodly house' of four storeys, where the noble patients stayed. Lettice wrote, 'Faythefull, faultelesse, yet sumway unfortunatt, yet must suffer.' One of Mary's messages, scratched in French, declared that 'God alone who of my heart has cognizance will one day render clear my innocence'. Her longest-serving custodian, the Earl of Shrewsbury, had a daughter-in-law who was also Queen Katherine Parr's niece – Lady Anne Talbot inscribed on the window a heartfelt observation, 'Fortune is to me somtyme a mother, somtyme a stepdame'.

Lettice's mother, Catherine Carey, was the daughter of Mary Boleyn and so she too was the niece of a Queen, Anne Boleyn. She was one of the maternal relatives who became Elizabeth I's closest personal friends – the only member of this side of the family who was neither 'faythefull' nor 'faultelesse' in Good Queen Bess's eyes was Lettice herself. And Elizabeth certainly endeavoured to make sure that she was 'sumway unfortunatt, yet must suffer'! Lettice was derided as the 'She-Wolf' who incurred Elizabeth's implacable anger.

The reason was that this beautiful, ambitious cousin trod on forbidden territory in 1578, by marrying a nobleman who had long 'forborne marriage in respect of Her Majesty's displeasure'. Robert Dudley, Earl of Leicester, was still accorded Elizabeth's affectionate nickname of her 'Eyes', but he had despaired years before of ever becoming her husband. Yet he had also felt much inhibited by the dread of her anger over his ultra-quiet wedding ceremony with Lettice.

Elizabeth lived up to all his fears of her over-reaction, with 'extreme choler' and 'great oaths', when she found out. She immediately banished the couple from Court, a disgrace which was permanent for Lettice, who compounded the situation with a flamboyant lack of repentance. Tidings came to Queen Elizabeth that the new Countess of Leicester sought to outdo her with magnificent clothes, and a rich coach and accompanying retinue of ladies. If Lettice gained huge satisfaction from such outward display, it was only temporary. She made the mistake of underestimating the sheer genius and ability of Elizabeth, qualities far more profound than surface ostentation.

Lettice's first husband, Walter Devereux, Earl of Essex, had often been absent from home on military duties, so her strong personality had been the main parental influence on the characters of their children. She was a role model for her two glamorous daughters, Penelope and Dorothy, who both showed boldness in flouting convention. Her effect on her eldest son, Robert, who succeeded to the earldom of Essex while still a boy, was to cosset him into an over-indulged, arrogant young man. His mother 'dearliest' loving him, and describing herself as she that 'hath made you the chief comfort of her life', when he was a grown man, had a tendency still to play on his emotions and treat him as a child in his early thirties.

Robert, Earl of Essex, filled the role of Queen's favourite after his stepfather Robert, Earl of Leicester, died. Elizabeth found, however, that his volatile temperament made their relationship far more stormy than she had experienced with her 'Eyes'. She forgave him many times, but he repeated his mother's error of misjudging her greatness as Queen. His version of defying her was the failed Essex Rebellion of 1600, which brought about his death under the executioner's axe early the next year. Lettice's third husband, Christopher Blount, was also beheaded for his involvement.

This background of rebellion in the close family circle of the 'She-Wolf' combined with one of piracy and smuggling in that of Anne, Duchess of Somerset, to bring about joint descendants of theirs, who include Queen Elizabeth II. Both their eldest sons were the next links in the lines of descent which led to this merging of their family trees, when Lettice's granddaughter, Frances Devereux, married Anne's great-grandson, William Seymour. Frances was not quite seventeen months old when rebel Robert, her father, was executed. She was named after her mother, whose own father was another eminent Elizabethan with a royal nickname – Sir Francis Walsingham, chief of the secret service, was the Queen's 'Moor' because of his swarthy looks. As for nicknames in William Seymour's ancestry, his mother, Honora Rogers, gained the curious title of 'Onus Blowze' amid a tangle of family ties which made her the sister-in-law and later, but simultaneously, the daughter-in-law of the same Seymour. Her reluctant in-law was himself known as 'Little Hertford' at Elizabeth's Court, due to his diminutive stature. Edward, Earl of Hertford, had been head of the Seymour family since his early teens, however, and he much disapproved of Honora.

The matriarch, Duchess Anne, was literally more accommodating. The romances which led to secret marriages for both her heir, Lord Hertford, and his elder son, Edward, Lord Beauchamp, had begun under her roof at Hanworth. The social gulf between their wives was very wide, though, for her son had aimed high by matching himself in 1560 with a Tudor princess in line for the throne, his beloved Lady Catherine Grey. In contrast, her grandson had opted to marry beneath his rank in 1582 and chose this daughter of a Dorset knight, Sir Richard Rogers, who was known to encourage pirates and smugglers.

Honora Rogers had been welcomed into Anne's household at Hanworth after the marriage of her eldest brother Andrew – some fifteen years her senior – to the Duchess's daughter, Mary. The age gap between Honora and Andrew placed them in the situation of anomaly that they were each the same age as their Seymour spouses, who nevertheless belonged to different generations of the family. Their second son, William, eventually became Earl and later, the Marquis of Hertford, and lived long enough to be restored to the Lord Protector's title of Duke of Somerset.

Lettice, Countess of Leicester, survived her cherished son, Essex, by the same number of years as his age at his execution – thirty-three. She lived at her Staffordshire manor, Drayton Bassett, near Tamworth, where she was said to be sprightly enough 'to walk a mile in the morning' when she was ninety-two. In 1634, she died there at the remarkable age for those days of ninety-four. Her property at Drayton later passed into the ownership of her granddaughter Frances, Duchess of Somerset. The lively, vivacious 'She-Wolf' Lettice would probably have approved of its use in modern times as Drayton Manor theme park and zoo.

CHAPTER 10

More Long-Lived Ladies

A shadowy figure called Mother Shipton is reputed to have inhabited the appropriately gloomy cave named after her at Knaresborough in Yorkshire. She was supposed to have been a contemporary of all five Tudor monarchs, and a prophetess or witch who was fortunate enough to die a natural death before the severe laws against witchcraft were passed. A small species of moth is named 'Mother Shipton' too, because the dark brown markings on its upper pair of wings resemble the facial profile of a witch!

'Mother Shipton' moth

The numerous prophecies attributed to Mother Shipton include the oft-quoted:

> *'Carriages without horses shall go*
> *And accidents fill the world with woe;*
> *Around the world thoughts shall fly*
> *In the twinkling of an eye.'*

The first printed appearance of this during the railway era of the 19th century caused some scepticism with regard to its authenticity, for instance from contributors to the journal *Notes and Queries* in 1872. A notice in the issue of April 1873 revealed that 'in a letter' to the journal 'Mr Charles Hindley of Brighton has made a clean breast of having fabricated the Prophecy ... with some ten others in his reprint of a cheapbook version, published in 1862'.

Even so, Hindley's so-called Mother Shipton prediction predated cars, telephones and 20th-century technological advances. As the author of *Yorkshire Legends and Traditions*, Thomas Parkinson, wrote in 1889: 'Few names of Yorkshire celebrities have gained more wide notoriety than Mother Shipton. It may be taken as tolerably certain that such a person was born in the neighbourhood of Knaresborough and lived at the period assigned to her.'

The 'usually accepted' year of her birth has been given as 1486. 'Her mother Agatha died in giving her birth' amid the 'strange and horrible noises' which 'attended her entry into the world, that the persons present were sorely tempted to fly from the place'. She was baptized as Ursula Sotheil, 'very morose and big bon'd, her head very long, with very great goggling but sharp and fiery eyes; her nose of an incredible and improportionable length, having in it many crooks and turnings, adorned with many strange pimples of divers colors, as red, blue, and mix't, which like vapors of brimstone, gave such a lustre to her affrighted spectators in the dead-time of the night ... that her nurse needed no other light to assist her in the performance of her duty ...'

Despite Ursula Sotheil's hideous face and crooked, misshapen body, however, 'her understanding was extraordinary'. Her luminous nose and goggling eyes may have been useful assets in her gloomy cave. The narrow approach to it, though, past the Wishing Well and Dropping Well, along the path ledged on the steep side of a gorge, would have been a challenge to someone of her ungainly and shambling gait.

Another name for the Dropping Well is the Petrifying Well, because objects immersed in the water flowing down the cliff there are coated in limestone. But to people who were scared of encountering Mother Shipton, its alternative name had a double meaning. An 18th-century folk song about her even referred to 'quaint goblins' hobbling round her at 'the famous dropping well'!

'One Toby Shipton, of Shipton, near York' is said to have married Ursula Sotheil early in Henry VIII's reign. If her fame as a fortune-teller then spread in the area around York, contemporary records do not mention this. She was alleged, for instance, to have foretold that Cardinal Wolsey 'might see York, but never come at it' and he vowed to burn her at the stake.

The first-hand biography of Wolsey by his gentleman-usher, George Cavendish, detailed closely his daily life during his final months in 1530. Cavendish wrote with an insider's knowledge, which gave him the chance to tell of Mother Shipton's prophecy and Wolsey's reaction, but his vivid account of his master did not allude to any such matters. Wolsey certainly never entered York, for he was arrested eight miles away at Cawood Castle on a charge of treason, a few days before he was to be installed as Archbishop in York Minster. Part of a 'fine stall ... of gold, pearl and precious stones' built for him there was reputed to have been presented to the King, at Mother Shipton's bidding.

If this was a sign of her extraordinary understanding, she fulfilled the role of a Tudor wise-woman indeed. She apparently survived to reach her three score years and ten during 'Bloody' Mary's reign, no mean achievement for a prophetess with a long nose who lived through such times of upheaval. In one of the traditions about her, she was credited with foretelling the date of her own death 'long before' it occurred in 1561 – the third year of Elizabeth's reign. The law against witchcraft passed two years later therefore posed no danger to Mother Shipton, but it began the persecution of English witches which lasted into the early 18th century.

The Prophesie of Mother Shipton was published in 1641, eighty years after her death, and was an immediate bestseller. Many further editions followed as time passed, but many also are the historians who have pointed out the tendency for her prophecies to be quoted after an event, crisis or disaster has gone by. Belief in an unfulfilled prophecy attributed to her - that England would return to the Roman Catholic faith – lingered in Norfolk, however, until the 19th century. Whatever view is taken of Mother Shipton, this mysterious character of myth and legend is part of the heritage of Tudor times.

One of Yorkshire's several neighbouring counties, Cheshire, had an even longer-lived lady who was also associated with an insect. Margaret Broadhurst of Hedge Row, near the village of Rainow, did not have a moth named after her, but was known locally as 'the cricket of the hedge' and she called her sixty year old daughter 'that snicket'. Having very little idea of her own true age, she claimed to have been eighty years old when she had her daughter! Records tell, though, that Margaret was born in 1546 and died when she was 104.

Two centenarian ladies from other counties outlived even this: Barbara Ashby of Lowesby in Leicestershire died in 1598, aged 105, and Mary Everton, who has a brass memorial in Battisford Church, Suffolk, reached the same age a decade later. Several Elizabethan parish registers include the names of yet more ladies from different areas:

> 1586, at Swainswick, Somerset: 'Elianor Cox, widow,
>   being an hundred yeres
> old, was buried the 8th day of Julie'.
> 1591, at Aston by Birmingham: 'Ould Weddowe Seye
>   was buried 30 March a
> woman of a hundredth years olde & more'.
> 1597, at St Peter's. Cornhill, London: '14 March.
>   Margery Mane widow, old,
> yet devout in often hearing ye word, [bur.] in ye cros
>   ile, (years) 100'.

This last entry implies some consideration for the frailty

of old age, but no such sympathy was shown to two Essex women who were brought before Church courts to answer charges of absence from compulsory attendance at Sunday services. In 1580, Joan Lawrence, aged ninety-one, told the court that her physical infirmity prevented her from walking almost a mile along a 'foul' trackway to attend her parish church at Colne Engaine. Anne Wilson, aged 'over eighty years old' in 1591, asserted that her age and state of health, and not 'contempt', caused her non-attendance at Weeley Church.

Difficulties with travelling led to the first written record of a carriage *with* horses – mentioned as a 'coche' - only five years before Mother Shipton died, so these vehicles must have been unusual sights around the time of that famous prophecy associated with her about 'carriages without horses'. In July 1556, a family friend invited Lady Mildred Cecil and her husband, Sir William, to visit him and offered: 'Peradventure my lady … cannot ride. Thereto I will provide this remedy – to send her my coche, because she shall have the less travail thither.' Mildred was then pregnant with her daughter, Ann.

Around the time of the Armada three decades later, the Cecil family suffered personal tragedy behind this great event, with the deaths of William Cecil's mother, wife and daughter in consecutive years. The 'happy mother of that most honourable Sir William Cecil, Lord Burghley' is commemorated next to his tomb in St Martin's Church, Stamford, Lincolnshire. She was Jane Heckington, from a local family, and she lived to see five generations of her descendants before her death in 1587, aged eighty-seven. Burghley House became the Cecils' property through her.

Leicester Cathedral contains a memorial to another matriarch – Mary Herrick, a former Lady Mayoress of Leicester, who survived long enough to know 'her children's children's children and their children to a total of 142 descendants'. She died aged ninety-seven in 1611. Mary was therefore in her teens when Cardinal Wolsey died at Leicester Abbey, attended by his loyal servant and biographer, George Cavendish. While Mary was in her early thirties, another local event took place, which involved the marriage of his brother, Sir William Cavendish, to a young Derbyshire widow who was then a lady-in-waiting to the Grey family at nearby Bradgate Park. His bride became renowned in history as Bess of Hardwick and is said to have been chosen by him 'chiefly for her beauty'.

But Sir William Cavendish acquired much more than beauty in the ambitious, materialistic Bess, after their wedding ceremony at two o'clock one morning of August 1547 in the chapel at Bradgate, with little Lady Jane Grey as one of the bleary-eyed bridesmaids. This was the second of Bess's marriages, and it marked a milestone and rise in status for her, as well as being the only one to produce children. Three sons and three daughters survived to adulthood. She had ambitions for them and also herself, so her domineering character emerged into the open with full strength during her Cavendish marriage. Her natural aptitude for business and building matters developed much expertise from her husband, a wealthy financial official who had been much involved in closing abbeys and priories during the Dissolution.

The following near-contemporary description of her was an attempt to malign a successful, competent woman with expressions of misogyny and envy: 'she was a woman of masculine understanding and conduct; proud, furious, selfish and unfeeling; a buyer and seller of estates, a money-lender, a farmer and a merchant of lead, coals and timber'. The known facts also show, however, that this view of Bess was fairly accurate! Her business mentor and husband, Sir William Cavendish, took part in some dishonest dealings, such as fiddling accounts for his own gain, during the Dissolution. Bess of Hardwick was a brilliant pupil under his guidance and influenced the choice of Chatsworth in her native Derbyshire as the Cavendishes' main home.

Bess's third husband, Sir William St Loe, even addressed her as 'my honest, sweet Chatsworth'. To her fourth husband, the Earl of Shrewsbury, it was 'my wife's house'.

The St Loe marriage lasted about five years, leaving Bess with most of his property, to the dismay of his own family. Her connections with royal ladies, including the Greys, continued during these marriages. She treated Lady Catherine Grey with great disdain when the news of Catherine's secret marriage was confided to her. Queen Elizabeth still had Bess imprisoned briefly in the Tower after this, however, and the ominous instruction to the Lieutenant to 'put her in awe of divers matters' during interrogations possibly hints at the threat of torture.

Bess's conduct towards Lady Catherine proved to be practice for her future treatment of the other main claimant to Elizabeth's throne, Mary Queen of Scots. In 1568, Bess rose further in status, when her fourth marriage made her the Countess of Shrewsbury. All appeared to go well at first, but in the following year, her new husband was appointed as custodian of the captive Queen of Scots. As time went by, some people unfavourably disposed towards Bess used puns on her noble title of Shrewsbury with 'shrew'. The following 'time-worn adage' was quoted by a bishop sympathizing with her husband: 'There is but one shrew in the world and every man hath her.'

Embroideries by Bess of Hardwick and Mary Queen of Scots, on display at Oxburgh Hall in Norfolk, date from the early part of Mary's years with the Shrewsburys. The teamwork involved in a creative project of this scale indicates some harmony then existed between them. Bess could be very congenial company, according to one of Elizabeth's courtiers who was pleasantly surprised to 'fynd no faulte with her ladyship', after anticipating that she would 'spit out venom' when she visited the Court!

A letter written by a royal Tudor lady in 1574 contained a personal glimpse of a very purposeful Bess, soon after several dramatic days in her company. 'On my going to Rufford Abbey, to my Lady of Shrewsbury,' stated Lady Margaret Douglas, Countess of Lennox, 'both being thereunto earnestly requested, and the place being not one mile distant out of my way ... and my Lady meeting me

Lady Margaret Douglas

herself upon the way, I could not well refuse … it was well known to all the country thereabouts that great provision was made for me …'

Bess had in tow her only unmarried daughter, Elizabeth Cavendish, who had been offered unsuccessfully to 'sundry' noblemen's sons as a potential bride. Lady Margaret Douglas was accompanied by her teenage son, Charles Stuart, Earl of Lennox. She admitted that she found him difficult to control. He was of higher rank, though, than any of the other young men who had rejected Bess's favourite daughter.

Lady Margaret wrote that she had been 'desirous … to have a match for him other than' Elizabeth Cavendish, but he 'entangled himself so that he could have none other …' She described the nuptials of the young couple during her stay at Rufford, in Nottinghamshire, as 'that hasty marriage'. Her cordial hostess Bess viewed the situation with more satisfaction, having now gained royal family ties of her own, in addition to her wealth and power.

Love was certainly not in the air when Queen Elizabeth found out about this whirlwind match without her consent! Bess's husband was swift to dissociate himself from the events at Rufford, declaring that 'it was dealt in suddenly, without my knowledge' and Bess, finding that the 'young gentleman was inclined to love with a few days' acquaintance, did her best to further her daughter to this match …' Bess and Lady Margaret were both imprisoned for a few months in the Tower.

Lady Margaret's words of lament almost summed up her life story: 'Thrice have I been cast into prison, not for matters of treason, but for love matters. First, when Thomas Howard, son of the Duke of Norfolk, was in love with myself; then for the love of Henry Darnley, my son, to Queen Mary of Scotland; and lastly, for the love of Charles, my younger son, to Elizabeth Cavendish.' As a young woman at the time of her romance with Lord Thomas Howard in the 1530s, Lady Margaret was one of the most beautiful of her generation. Love poems which they wrote to each other were included in a collection of Tudor poetry known as the *Devonshire Manuscript*.

Inscriptions on her altar-tomb in Westminster Abbey detail her important dynastic position in the family trees of the Tudor and Stuart monarchs: 'This ladye had to her great-grandfather King Edward 4, to her grandfather King Henry 7, to her uncle King Henry 8, to her cousin-germane King Edward 6, to her brother King James of Scotland the 5, to her grandchild King James 6 … having to her great-grandmother and grandmother two queens, both named Elizabeth, to her mother Margaret Queen of Scots, to her aunt Mary ye Frenche Queen, to her cousins-germanes, Mary and Elizabeth, Queens of England.'

She was also 'daughter and sole heire of Archibald, Earl of Angus, by Margaret Queen of Scotland (… eldest daughter to Henry 7th)' and 'beare unto Matthew, Earl of Lennox, her husband, 4 sons and 4 daughters. Henry, second sonne to this lady, and father to James VI … was murdered at the age of 21 years …'

Although Margaret Douglas was born in England in 1515, she was sometimes called 'The Princess of Scotland'. To Henry VIII she had been 'niece Marget' and to her husband, 'sweet Madge'. She had briefly been the first lady in the land when her corpulent royal uncle was in between his third and fourth wives, and his own daughters, Mary and Elizabeth, had been declared illegitimate.

King Henry VII had foreseen the possibility of the crowns of England and Scotland being united by the descendants of Margaret Tudor, Queen of Scots. As eldest granddaughter to the first Tudor King, and grandmother of the first Stuart King of England, Lady Margaret Douglas helped this to become a reality.

To Bess of Hardwick, Lady Margaret's exalted ties of kinship might have seemed almost as long as the Great North Road, along which she was travelling when Bess escorted her as a guest to Rufford Abbey. But to Lady Margaret herself, all her royal blood had not prevented an accusation of theft once being attempted against her for selling wood, lead and stones from the ruins of Jervaulx Abbey in Yorkshire, to help support a household appropriate to her rank at Temple Newsam, near Leeds, and Settrington in East Yorkshire.

These houses and the former abbey were amongst estates confiscated from rebel leaders executed after the Pilgrimage of Grace, and granted by Henry VIII to Lady Margaret and her husband on their marriage in 1544. She had been en route to visit Settrington when she stopped at Rufford. Her journey had already been halted further south, as she said, to rest her 'overlaboured mules' which were 'both crooked and lame'. The irony was that Lady Margaret was so impoverished when she encountered the lower-ranking Bess of Hardwick. Yet Bess then had the opportunity at another old monastery, Rufford, to put on an ostentatious display of her own wealth, partly accumulated by the fraudulent activities of her second husband during the suppression of the abbeys and priories.

Margaret Douglas had recently reached the age of fifty-nine, and at the time she was only the second member of the Tudor dynasty to live beyond fifty-six – the other being her

Jervaulx Abbey, North Yorkshire

great-grandmother, Lady Margaret Beaufort, who survived till her mid-sixties.

The achievement of living this long was remarkable for Margaret Douglas, considering the chequered life she had led. Close and sustaining friends such as her cousin, Queen Mary Tudor, and Mary Howard, Duchess of Richmond, had died long before. Six of her eight children did not survive infancy, and of the two sons who did so, her beloved elder son, Lord Darnley, second husband of Mary Queen of Scots, was murdered by conspirators including some of her Douglas relatives who had received hospitality from her at Temple Newsam. Her husband was assassinated while he was ruling as Regent of Scotland for their grandson, King James.

One relative not mentioned on Lady Margaret's tomb pedigree was James's mother and her own niece and former daughter-in-law, the captive Queen of Scots, who was imprisoned at Chatsworth, about twenty miles away, during the Rufford rendezvous. Before travelling north, Margaret had asked Queen Elizabeth whether she might accept an invitation to Chatsworth if she received one. She wrote that Elizabeth's reply was to 'pray me not, lest it be thought I should agree with the Queen of Scots'. Margaret's vehement response to this, 'I could never forget the murder of my child', found much favour with Elizabeth.

In the last few years of Lady Margaret's life, though, she was reconciled with Mary. She 'fully and freely acknowledged the innocence' of Mary over Darnley's murder and 'asked her pardon for the injury she had suffered from her long and cruel accusations'. Their increased friendliness came about, partly through the gentle influence of Margaret's new daughter-in-law, Elizabeth Cavendish, who had been on affectionate terms with Mary, if not with her own mother Bess. The main reason, however, was the birth of a daughter, Lady Arabella Stuart in 1575, a year after the 'hasty marriage'.

The captive Queen enjoyed her occasional visits from her 'niece Arbelle' and gave the little girl many gifts. But while

Arabella's arrival in the world brought Mary to more amity with one grandmother, Lady Margaret, it had a divisive effect with the other. Bess of Hardwick was exuberant at the acquisition of a royal grandchild and also defiant of criticism that her ambition had driven her to aim too high. After all, in Bess's estimation, her daughter Elizabeth was to blame for the secret nuptials at Rufford.

Bess's rash remark that her granddaughter, Arabella, had a better claim to the English throne, 'not being an alien by birth like Mary and her son', caused deep offence to Mary Queen of Scots.

Both of Arabella's parents died in their twenties. Bess of Hardwick apparently shed copious tears of grief for the daughter who had once expressed, in a letter to her, distress at being the recipient of some maternal 'displeasure' after the marriage. Lady Margaret Douglas found that she had endured one family tragedy too many with the loss of her only remaining son and went into a 'languishing decay', before she died suddenly in March 1578, aged sixty-two. She became the third longest lived of the Tudors, after Queen Elizabeth I and Lady Margaret Beaufort.

Bess was left with the full guardianship of a 'precious jewel' – Arabella. Evidently, Bess had already instilled fear into some of her other grandchildren, for their parents threatened them with a visit from 'Lady Grandmother' if they misbehaved! The future did not augur well for a lively, high-spirited girl such as Arabella being brought up by an ageing Bess the boss half a century her senior. Queen Elizabeth much approved of this arrangement, which was cost-effective from her point of view, although the domestic battles in the Shrewsbury household had become increasingly acrimonious due to the breakdown of Bess's marriage.

The Queen tried to negotiate a truce between the warring couple, but the Earl of Shrewsbury adamantly refused to heal the rift with his 'evil and wicked wife'. This usually mild-mannered man further called Bess a 'demon' and 'burdensome charge'. She and two of her sons had spread untrue rumours that he and his other 'charge' and 'demon', Mary Queen of Scots, had had an affair. There were also bitter property disputes over Chatsworth and the 'great expence' of Bess's grandiose building work there.

In north-east Derbyshire, Bess had an important property which was undoubtedly hers. The estate of the small manor house at Hardwick, where she was born, provided timber for the building of Chatsworth. She had bought it from her brother in the 1570s to help him to clear his debts, and in the mid-1580s she moved in there herself and began enlarging the manor house into what is now Hardwick Old Hall. Bess took ten year old Arabella with her to Hardwick and all contact with Mary Queen of Scots ceased. Arabella never saw her kindly royal aunt again – she was now completely under the domination of Bess.

A life of surveillance and restriction, and of sleeping in the same bedchamber as her grandmother till her mid-twenties, was the prospect which awaited Arabella. Bess believed that not only was she the grandmother-guardian of a royal princess, but of England's next Queen – a most prestigious position which required appropriately splendid accommodation at Hardwick.

Bess's work on the Old Hall was meant to impress visitors, especially from the Court of the Queen who shared her name. She was also using this as an opportunity to let the world know that although she was a woman, she could achieve such display without her husband. The Old Hall was still unfinished when Bess was again a widow in 1590. True to form, she swiftly took full control of all her lands and her widow's jointure of a third of the vast Shrewsbury properties. Within weeks of her husband's death, one of the finest Elizabethan mansions, Hardwick New Hall, was begun. And *this* was intended to receive and entertain a far greater person than any noble courtier – the Queen herself!

On the pinnacles of the four-storied building, the initials 'ES', for Elizabeth Shrewsbury, and her Countess's coronet stand out against the skyline. The enormous windows are progressively larger from the ground floor to the

Bess's monogram on a tower at Hardwick Hall, Derbyshire

magnificent state apartments on the second. Bess was almost seventy when her prodigy house was completed in 1596, but it reflected all her independence and power as the wealthiest woman in England after Queen Elizabeth.

Arabella, though, was denied any personal freedom of movement during those years of intensive building at Hardwick, and her feeling of being in prison strengthened as walls grew ever higher. She made occasional visits to Court, which brought some respite from her grandmother's authority and a rare chance to enjoy the much more congenial company of people of her own age group. Arabella found each return to Hardwick and Bess's strict supervision increasingly difficult. She once went on hunger strike and declared that she would not eat until she left Hardwick.

After various thwarted escape plans, her uncle Henry Cavendish – 'my bad son Henry', according to Bess – attempted to rescue Arabella in March 1603. His failure did at least prompt Queen Elizabeth to sanction Arabella's removal from Hardwick and Bess. The 'Virgin Queen' never travelled far enough north to visit Hardwick, and as

Arabella was in the process of leaving there, the news broke that Elizabeth had died, after reigning for 'forty-four years, four months and seven days'.

Arabella was then the only English princess of royal blood and should have been Chief Mourner at Elizabeth's funeral. But she refused to perform this duty, saying that as she had been kept from the Queen for much of her life, she would not 'now come near her in death'. Arabella only ever went back to Hardwick once. Bess disinherited her and Henry Cavendish, but lived her own twilight years under the cloud of knowing that her unlimited ambition had ultimately backfired on her. Bess's reward for success in acquiring and investing in a royal grandchild was Arabella's hatred of 'Lady Grandmother' for so ruling her life.

Local tradition in Derbyshire foretold that Bess would not die while she was involved with building projects, but when the severe winter of 1607-8 brought a halt to these, she died on 13 February 1608 at the age of eighty. Whether or not this story is true, Bess had her own monument erected in the Cavendish Chapel in Derby Cathedral and her epitaph rightly says that her buildings were 'highly distinguished for their magnificence'.

The Countess's coronet adorns the tomb effigy of Bess, who was linked in death with the anniversaries of five queens. She died sixty-six years to the day after the execution of Queen Catherine Howard in 1542, fifty-four years since that of Lady Jane Grey on 12 February 1554, twenty-one years after Mary Queen of Scots was beheaded on 8 February 1587, over a century after the death of Queen Elizabeth of York on 11 February 1502 and ninety-two years since the birth of Queen Mary Tudor on 16 February 1516. Added to that, forty-one years had passed since the murder of the Queen of Scots' second husband and Lady Margaret Douglas's beloved son, Lord Darnley, on 10 February 1567 – the same day as the fourth birthday of the younger son of Elizabeth Cavendish's godmother, Lady Catherine Grey!

Arabella secretly married Lady Catherine's grandson, William Seymour, and as he was also a claimant to the

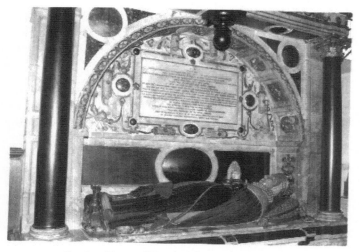

Tomb of Bess of Hardwick, Derby Cathedral

English throne, they were both imprisoned. She escaped from house arrest in north London, in an attempt to be reunited with him in France. William escaped from the Tower and arrived in Paris to await her, but unfortunately Arabella was recaptured and sent to the Tower, where she died in 1615. She was interred in Westminster Abbey, in the vault beneath the tomb of the aunt who had been so fond of her, Mary Queen of Scots. When William remarried, his eldest daughter was named Arabella, in honour of her. He erected Lady Catherine's tomb in the Lady Chapel of Salisbury Cathedral.

A short distance from this, on the other side of the Cathedral nave is the monument of the long-lived lady who *was* the Chief Mourner at Queen Elizabeth's funeral. In a contemporary illustration of the procession behind the deceased Queen's coffin, her friend Helena, Marchioness of Northampton, was depicted with her handkerchief at the ready. Helena was then ranked as the next 'in nobilitie' after Lady Arabella and her tears for Elizabeth were genuinely heartfelt. Like her English noble title, her maiden name was also long – Helena Ulfsdotter Snakenborg was born into a Swedish noble family in 1549. She was befriended by Queen Elizabeth soon after her arrival in England as a 'young and fair' maid of honour to Princess Cecilia, sister of one of Elizabeth's suitors, Eric of Sweden.

Cecilia came to the royal Tudor Court on behalf of her brother, to seek favour for his hopes of marrying Elizabeth. Helena found some marriage hopes of her own when the brother of another English Queen fell in love with her. William Parr, by then raised to the rank of Marquess of Northampton, had retained Queen Elizabeth's affection, in honoured memory of her much-loved stepmother, Queen Katherine Parr. He was thirty-six years older than the teenage Helena, but she wrote to her widowed mother in Sweden of her affectionate feelings towards him, possibly seeing him as a father-figure.

Elizabeth's habitual fondness for the Parr family extended to Helena and royal approval for her marriage to William Parr was given, a rare example of such support from the 'Virgin Queen'. Princess Cecilia approved at first, then disapproved, but Helena refused to end her relationship with him. She settled in England for the rest of her life, never returning to her native land. Elizabeth appointed her as a Lady of the Privy Chamber and usually referred to Helena as 'the good Lady Marquess' after her marriage.

The Elizabethan writer, William Camden, hinted that Helena lived up to the Queen's name for her, in making her husband happy during their short marriage and his life 'sweetly ended'. He left property and money to his young widow, who continued in her privileged place at Court. Helena's first spouse was noted for his love of dogs. When she remarried, her second husband was a knight so skilled in riding horses that he took part in one of the earliest recorded races and has a horse at the foot of his effigy on their tomb. Sir Thomas Gorges served Elizabeth as a Groom of the Privy Chamber and was about twelve years older than Helena. He had gained royal favour towards his courtship of her, but this began with an entanglement that neither of them envisaged. When they danced together at a ball one night, Helena found that her train became tangled round his legs, almost causing a fall!

Twists and turns of a different kind swirled around their courtship and marriage. The Queen expressed amusement at Sir Thomas's fears that there was no chance of romance after that dance, and she told him not to give up hope. Later, when the prospect of a wedding between Helena and Sir Thomas approached, Elizabeth suddenly reverted to her usual opposition to marriage and refused to sanction theirs. A familiar pattern then set in, as they added to the large number of people who married secretly in Elizabeth's reign, without her permission, and faced her fury and retribution. They were both banished from Court, Helena to the Gorges' London town house, Sir Thomas to prison in the Tower.

Elizabeth faced a dilemma when she received news of Helena's 'extreme anguish of a sorrowful mind', and her impassioned pleas to be allowed to return to Court. Wives who were excluded from the Court of Queen Elizabeth usually continued to be excluded. Yet sending her 'good Lady Marquess' away had been Elizabeth's personal loss too. The bonds of friendship between them were genuine and mutual, and Elizabeth knew Helena well enough to realize that her words about her suffering were sincere. Nor was there any threat to the Tudor throne from the newly-weds. The Queen relented, reinstated them at Court and her friendship with Helena resumed so strongly that sumptuous New Year gifts were exchanged in future.

Helena's first child was a daughter, born in 1578, and named Elizabeth after her godmother, the Queen. Elizabeth Gorges was also destined to become a long-lived lady - she survived her two younger sisters and five brothers by several years, and reached the age of eighty-one.

The family home at Longford in Wiltshire was bought by Helena and Sir Thomas in the late 1570s, when it was a small manor house. They replaced this building with a triangular-shaped mansion called Longford Castle during the 1580s, and it was praised by a Tudor diarist as a 'faire new house of stone' with the 'fairest garden and greene walks ... that I have seen ... it is much spent in pantreyes'. These last words indicate that Helena herself influenced its design. Part of her motive in its construction was to provide luxury accommodation in the area for Queen Elizabeth, not so much for impressive display like with Bess of Hardwick's houses, but out of concern for the Queen's welfare and comfort. During a visit to the manor house at Longford in 1574, Elizabeth had been unable to escape from a downpour of torrential rain, due to the lack of space there.

Although no records exist of a royal return to Longford, Elizabeth is believed to have been entertained by Helena and her family at their Castle, and even, according to one Tudor tale, to have contributed to its cost with some treasure trove. Funds for the building work were running low by the Armada summer of 1588. Sir Thomas Gorges served then in Hampshire as the Governor of Hurst Castle, on its narrow strip of land opposite the Isle of Wight and famous sea stacks called the Needles. When a Spanish galleon was wrecked, Helena petitioned Elizabeth to grant her the hull, so that Longford Castle could be completed with money raised from the sale of this part of the huge ship. Her request was granted and the wreckage of the hull was later found to contain bars of silver and iron, along with hidden treasure.

The work at Longford Castle was duly done by 1591. In the same year, the poet Edmund Spenser dedicated his poem *Daphnaida* to Helena, because the young Dorset lady commemorated in this was 'in affection greatly devoted unto your Ladiship'. She had a rather unusual name for a girl – Douglas – and came from the Howard family. Her husband was Sir Thomas Gorges' nephew, Arthur, who was depicted in the poem as grief-stricken at her death while she was still in her teens.

The 'good Lady Marquess', however, lived till she was eighty-six. The attractive qualities of Helena's character, which Elizabeth had quickly recognized, shone through with some of the generous bequests she made in her will –

such as a legacy to the poor of Wraxall, her husband's birthplace near Bristol, and another to Mary Ellis, 'whose grandmother nursed my late husband, Sir Thomas Gorges'.

Another lady who showed concern for Queen Elizabeth's welfare was Magdelan Dacre, Viscountess Montague. Her houses at Battle Abbey and Cowdray in Sussex were such centres of the Roman Catholic faith that they were known as 'Little Rome'. When Elizabeth heard that this former lady-in-waiting to her sister, Queen Mary, was praying for her, she asked one of her personal attendants, Lady Scudamore, to send a message of thanks: 'The Queen ... is persuaded she fareth much the better for your prayers, and therefore desireth you ever hereafter to be mindful of her in your prayers.' Elizabeth, with her natural asset of judging individual characters accurately, had esteemed the ability of Lady Magdelan's husband and employed him on diplomatic missions, despite his family's staunch Catholicism. His open loyalty 'to live or die in her defence' during the Armada, was recognized with a royal visit to Cowdray during the summer progress in 1591.

Lady Magdelan had originally made her debut at Court in 1554, when she was sixteen and walked in the wedding procession of Queen Mary Tudor and Philip of Spain. She repelled an attempted invasion by King Philip one day when she was washing her face and his arm reached in through an open window nearby. He received a sharp stroke on the offending arm with a staff wielded by Magdelan and subsequently treated her with respect!

Magdelan was the sister of Anne Dacre, Countess of Cumberland, and the great-aunt of the 'queen of the north', Lady Anne Clifford (both detailed in Chapter 1). In 1608, shortly before Bess of Hardwick died, Lady Magdelan reached her three score years and ten, but fell ill with palsy, which ended her earthly days during the following spring.

Eye-witness descriptions of her physical appearance in old age were that she was 'fat and gross' and very tall. Spiritually, though, Lady Magdelan was acknowledged as being head and shoulders above many people too, for her courage, piety and devotion to her religion. Having been on friendly terms with both the reigning Tudor Queens during her lifetime, her last resting place in the church of a former nunnery and near the tomb of a relative of the first Tudor monarch, may seem appropriate. At Easebourne Priory Church, adjacent to Cowdray House, lies Sir David Owen, an illegitimate uncle of King Henry VII, who was two years younger than his nephew.

The nuns of Easebourne were to benefit from several bequests in Sir David's will, dated 1529, including funds for the building of a private, covered passage between their convent and the church. But the small Augustinian nunnery was dissolved in 1536, during his lifetime. As the nuns left, the last sub-prioress was said to have placed a curse on the male heirs of future owners, which was apparently fulfilled over 250 years later.

Sub-prioresses of both Tudor and medieval times at Easebourne seem to have made themselves particular targets of criticism. Some of the nuns complained in 1521, for instance, that the sub-prioress was too strict. She rejoindered by alleging that they were too disobedient, and at the same time she divulged news of a naughty nun with the surname 'Covert', who had succumbed to temptation by a local farmer several years before! In the decade leading up to the Tudor period, a sub-prioress had been ordered by the Bishop of Chichester to be removed from her position. Naughty nuns had also been active then, with two of them who had borne children running away from the remote priory, accompanied by the chaplain.

A curious mixture of nuns, the Armada, Ireland, Spanish prisoners, the Queen and the husband of another of her long-lived, favourite ladies appeared in a blank verse, *A Tale of Two Swannes* by William Vallens in 1589:

> *'From Stansted unto Hodesdon goe these Swannes,*
> *From thence to Broxbourne, and to Wormley Wood,*
> *And so salute the holy house of Nunnes*
> *That late belonged to Captain Edward Dennie,*
> *A knight in Ireland of the best accompt,*

Who late make execution of our foes,
I meane of Spanyardes, that with open armes,
Attempted both against our queen and us.'

The journey of the two swans in this poem was along the River Lea in Hertfordshire. The nunnery was at Cheshunt – the Benedictine sisters there were reported to have received unauthorized visits in the evenings from monks of nearby Waltham Abbey in Essex. After the Dissolution, both these religious houses became properties of the Denny family. Sir Edward Denny was serving Queen Elizabeth in Ireland during the Armada, and when Spanish ships were wrecked in storms off the west coast of Ireland, his wife Margaret helped him in capturing Spanish prisoners.

The 'execution of our foes' mentioned in William Vallens' poem was carried out on her orders. During her husband's absence on government business, twenty-four enemy captives were brought to the Dennys' residence at Tralee Castle and she had them hanged.

Lady Denny came from the Edgcumbe family of Cotehele and Mount Edgcumbe in Cornwall. Her ancestors had fought on Henry VII's side at the Battle of Bosworth and remained staunchly loyal to the Tudor dynasty. Her mother, Margaret Luttrell, was a distant cousin of Anne Boleyn, so young Margaret Edgcumbe came to Queen Elizabeth's Court as a member already of the extended, and usually favoured, Boleyn family. She served as a maid-of-honour for five years until her marriage in 1583. A sure sign of affection for her was the wedding gift of richly embroidered gloves she received from the Queen – as well as the requisite royal approval. Sir Edward Denny was then a 'groom of Her Majestie's Privy Chamber', a position of trust which his father, Sir Anthony Denny, had held during her father's reign.

Queen Elizabeth's warship, the *Victory*, landed unexpectedly on the south-west coast of Ireland in December 1589, near Tralee. The ship was commanded by the Earl of Cumberland, Lady Anne Clifford's father, and had been driven by gale-force winds towards Ireland, after a maritime venture across the Atlantic. Margaret Denny returned to England with her husband and young family on the *Victory*, landing in her native Cornwall, at Falmouth.

Almost sixty years of life still lay ahead of her. The brass memorial to her in the chancel of Bishop's Stortford Church, Hertfordshire, states that she died in 1648, aged eighty-eight, and mentions her years as a maid of honour to 'Queen Elizabeth of blessed memory'. These last words of tribute to the great Tudor Queen were truly remarkable in being placed there forty-five years after her death – and at a time when England was only months away from beheading its Stuart monarch, Charles I, and becoming a republic.

But the Queen who had given her name to the Elizabethan Age and ruled her realm so successfully with her alternative names of 'Good Queen Bess' and 'Gloriana', was indeed 'of blessed memory' by the mid-17th century, after the disastrous years under the Stuarts.

And a year after the timeless tribute to her appeared on Lady Denny's epitaph, part of Elizabeth moved to the north of England, in the form of Lady Anne Clifford and began her renowned restoration work on her own domains. Lady Anne's early, formative experiences of seeing Elizabeth as an ageing, but powerful female ruler proved to be a profound and lasting influence on her.

The nautical theme of a posthumous tribute eventually to Lady Anne could equally have been said of Queen Elizabeth herself: 'Like him at the stern, she ... turned and steered the whole course of her affairs.'

Lady Anne Clifford – in her youth and aged 81

Bibliography

Ballinger, John. *'Katheryn of Berain'*, *Y Cymmrodor*, Vol.XL (1929)

Barron, Caroline M. (ed.) *Medieval London Widows, 1300-1500* (1994)

Bettey, J.H. *The Suppression of the Monasteries in the West Country* (1989)

Bradford, C.A. *Helena, Marchioness of Northampton* (1936)

Brown, William. *'Description of the Buildings of Twelve Small Yorkshire Priories'*, *Yorkshire Archaeological Journal*, Vol.IX (1890)

Calendar of Letters and Papers of the Reign of Henry VIII, Vols.XI to XV (1888-96)

Chadwick, S.J. *'Kirklees Priory'*, *Yorkshire Archaeological Journal*, Vol.XVI (1902)

Childs, Joy. *Tudor Derbyshire* (1985)

Clay, J.W. *'The Clifford Family'*, *Yorkshire Archaeological Journal*, Vol.XVIII (1905)

Yorkshire Monasteries: Suppression Papers (1912)

Clifford family. *Clifford Letters of the Sixteenth Century* (1962)

Councer, C.R. *'The Dissolution of the Kentish Monasteries'*, *Archaeologia Cantiana*, Vol.XLVII (1935)

Dawson, W.H. *History of Skipton* (1882)

Harvey, Nancy Lenz. *Elizabeth of York, Tudor Queen* (1973)

Hay, D. *'The Dissolution of the Monasteries in the Diocese of Durham'*, *Archaeologia Aeliana*, 4th series, Vol.XV (1938)

Hayes, Raymond H. *A History of Rosedale* (1970)

Hill, Pamela. *The Green Salamander* (1977)

Holles, Gervase. *Memorials of the Holles Family,1493-1656* (1937)

Jackson, J.E. *'Amye Robsart', Wiltshire Archaeological Journal,* Vol.XVII (1878)

Lipscomb, H.C. *History of Staindrop Church and its Monuments* (1888)

Living, H.G.D. *Records of Romsey Abbey* (1906)

Marshall, Emma. *Eventide Light* (1890)

Martienssen, Anthony. *Queen Katherine Parr* (1973)

Moss, Fletcher. *A History of the Old Parish of Cheadle, Cheshire* (1894)

Paul, John. *'Dame Elizabeth Shelley, Last Abbess of St Mary's Abbey, Winchester', Hampshire Field Club Proceedings,* Vol.23, pt.2 (1965)

Parkinson, Thomas. *Yorkshire Legends and Traditions* (1889)

Romsey Millenary Celebrations, A.D. 907 – A.D.1907 (1907)

Seymour, William. *Ordeal by Ambition* (1972)

Sheils, W.J. and Wood, Diana (eds.) *Women in the Church* (1990)

Smith, James. *Wilton and its Associations* (1851)

Southern, A.C. (ed.) *An Elizabethan Recusant House, Richard Smith's Life of the Lady Magdelan, Viscountess Montague (1538-1608)* (1954)

Sydenham, Laura. *Shaftesbury and its Abbey* (1959)

Tregellas, Walter H. *Cornish Worthies,* Vol.I (1884)

Victoria County History of Yorkshire, Vol.3 (1913)

Woodward, G.W.O. *Dissolution of the Monasteries* (1966)

Wright, T. (ed.) *Three Chapters of Letters on the Suppression of the Monasteries* (1843)

Wriosthesley, Charles. *A Chronicle of England during the Reigns of the Tudors* (1875, 1877)

Also by **Marie Sandeford**

The companion volume to LONG-LIVED LADIES
AND MORE TUDOR TALES

TALES OF TUDOR WOMEN

Tudor England was said to be 'the paradise of women'. Many found roles for themselves, although their lives were restricted and their opportunities limited.

Queens and heroines of romance, martyrs, rebels, gifted healers and craftswomen, businesswomen, bossy women – and even a roaring girl – all show in *Tales of Tudor Women* how they faced odds against them in an eventful and turbulent age …

'historians of early-modern women will find within it jewels of information.'

Women's History Magazine

ISBN 0 9534584 1 5   Paperback   120 pages   28 illustrations

Published by Joroby Books, 15 Bridgewater Drive,
Great Glen, Leics. LE8 9DX

Tales of Tudor Women can be ordered through U.K. bookshops, or direct from the publisher at the above address, price £6.50 plus post & packing.